Ted Blake
– an inspiration to leisure managers

KU-359-918

ACKNOWLEDGEMENTS

The Ted Blake Tribute Team acknowledges with thanks all contributors to the book. This free publication, for those within or entering the field of leisure management, could not have been contemplated without substantial funding and support in kind.

Doreen Blake, Ted's wife, son Tim, and Jean Mackenzie, Ted's lifetime Personal Assistant, gave us their support, encouragement and permission to go ahead with the project.

When Ted became ill, he talked about giving his library of transparencies to Roger Quinton. Sadly they both died before this was done, a double blow to the industry. Respecting his wishes, Doreen gave them to RQA – Roger's company, so that they could continue to be of value in leisure management training. With the kind co-operation and permission of Roger's widow, Liz, and David Lord, Managing Director of RQA, the Tribute Group were given unfettered access to this valuable resource. Many others provided us with tapes, handouts and articles, which added to the 'collection', and we thank Roy McLarty at the University of Hertfordshire for making the 'Blake Archive' available to us.

Our idea for the book was shared with Derek Casey, then Chief Executive of Sport England, through whom a grant covering half of the production costs was secured.

Alan Smith, then Chief Executive of The Institute of Leisure and Amenity Management, agreed that the Institute's contribution to the publication could be the design and production of the manuscript, a decision supported by his successor, Andy Worthington, a great fan of Ted Blake. The ILAM design team included: Jonathan Ives, Stephen Gray and Anne Henderson, to whom we extend our thanks for their patient and painstaking work and collaboration.

To all contributors and supporters of this unique – and complex – project, we say a huge thank you. We trust that, in some small measure, it serves as a lasting and fitting tribute to the inimitable Ted Blake.

George on behalf of:

The Tribute Team:

George Torkildsen	David Fisher
Gerry Carver	Geoff Gearing
Bernard Warden	John Birch
Hywel Griffiths	

1

Funding and Support

We acknowledge, with thanks, the contribution from so many people towards this publication, which illustrates the esteem in which Ted Blake was held. The overriding message, articulated by the late Jim Munn, was "Ted was an inspiration before his time".

Main sponsors of the book:
Sport England
Institute of Leisure and Amenity Management

Main sponsor from local authorities:
Leicester City Council

Corporate donors:
Training Systems (UK) Ltd
CCL Leisure
FaulknerBrowns
Cannons Leisure Management
Strategic Leisure Ltd.
PMP
DC Leisure Group
Roger Quinton Associates
L & R Consulting
David Fisher Leisure Ltd.
Second Innings
Torkildsen Barclay Leisure Management
Sports Project Services
Ploszajski Lynch Consulting

Associations, Institutions and Local Authorities:
The Recreation Managers Association of GB
Chief Leisure Officers Association
Institute of Sport & Recreation Management
ISRM Consultants
Runnymede Borough Council
Chiltern Leisure Trust
Guildford Spectrum

Individual Contributions:
Doreen Blake
Tim Blake
Jean Mackenzie
Peter Johnson
John Griffiths
Jim Munn
Kit Campbell
Liz Quinton
George Torkildsen
David Fisher
Gerry Carver
Geoff Gearing
Bernard Warden

John Birch
Hywel Griffiths
John Atkinson
Terry Marshall
Gwynne Griffiths
Gordon Bates
Dennis Hinds
Jim Lynch
Tom Clitherow
Paul Secher
Sue Tarling
Pat Kendall
Liz Terry

Contents

Published by

Institute of Leisure and Amenity Management

ILAM House, Lower Basildon, Reading, RG8 9NE

Tel: 01491 874800

ISBN 1 873903 97 9

Ted Blake
19.10.1921 – 6.3.1998

Biographical details

- Born in Edmonton, London, 19th October 1921.

- Attended Latymer Grammar School.

- Served as a Sergeant Major in the army during the Second World War.

- Married Doreen in 1942.

- Trained as a teacher at Forest Training College; Carnegie, Leeds and London University, gaining a Teachers Certificate; Diploma with distinction in Physical Education; and Diploma with distinction in Health Education.

- Practiced as a school teacher until 1956.

- Established a company – Nissen International – which became the largest UK manufacturer of gymnastic and recreation equipment. The company was sold in 1980.

- Became a management consultant and trainer and worked with over 150 local authorities and 500 companies.

- Ted was founder member of The British Trampoline Federation, organising the first world championships, safety conferences and other trampolining events.

- In 1975, he won a National Award of The Chartered Institute of Marketing for Outstanding Contributions to British Marketing.

- Ted was a:
  - Fellow of the Institute of Directors
  - Fellow of The Institute of Management
  - Fellow of The Physical Education Association
  - Hon. Fellow of The Institute of Leisure and Amenity Management
  - Companion of The Institute of Sport and Recreation Management
  - Fellow of The Recreation Managers Association
  - Member of The Chartered Institute of Marketing
  - Member of The Association of Management Education & Development

- Ted leaves behind a widow Doreen, son Tim, daughter Deborah and grandchildren Matthew and Gemma.

Memories, Reflections and Setting the Scene

Ted Blake's presentations on the achievement of excellence in management made a lasting impression on all who heard him. To Doreen, Ted's wife, and Jean, Ted's PA, their lasting impression is the use he made, and his love of, "The Impossible Dream", which was the first song he played in the first talk he gave for RECMAN, the Sports Council's annual conference, and which Ted called "The Leisure Manager's Quest".

When asked what he would like as his epitaph, Ted quoted what was printed at the bottom of his notepaper: "He helped people make better decisions". Our hope is that this book will help readers to do just that.

This book provides Ted Blake with a chance to make a first impression on a generation of leisure, sport and recreation managers and others working in the field who never met him or heard him deliver memorable conference papers. It also provides another opportunity for those of us who were fortunate enough to know him, to enjoy his humour, to gleen afresh his management insights and be inspired by him.

Ted Blake was a gifted teacher, a graduate of Carnegie College of Physical Education, Leeds. He was an Honorary Fellow of the Physical Education Association, Companion of the Institute of Sport and Recreation Management and Honorary Fellow of the Institute of Leisure and Amenity Management. Ted held the Diploma of Health Education with Distinction from London University. He was founder of the British Trampoline Federation, Fellow of the Institute of Directors, Fellow of the Institute of Management and Member of the Chartered Institute of Marketing. Ted left the teaching profession and set up the Nissen Trampoline Company in the UK, but as the company grew and became more involved in exporting, the name was changed to Nissen International. In 1975, the company won the Chartered Institute of Marketing National Award for outstanding contribution to British Marketing. When Ted left Nissen, he formed the company, Ted Blake Ltd, focussing on management and marketing training and consultancy which took him into areas additional to leisure, such as Housing Departments in local authorities, businesses, institutions and a variety of non-leisure organisations. He ended his professional career as a sought-after management trainer, keynote conference speaker and after-dinner raconteur. Ted's PA recalls him still dictating notes a couple of days before he died.

Ted Blake was one of the most outstanding contributors to the fledgling profession of Leisure Management in the United Kingdom. His initiatives, in partnership with Harry Littlewood, of the Sports Council, such as inaugurating the Recreation Management Conference, RECMAN, and the Sports Centre Management of the Year Award scheme, and his inspiration and his support, helped to galvanise the ad hoc network of agencies and organisations into an embryo profession with a vision of excellence in Leisure Management. It is fitting, therefore, that a major sponsor of this publication is Sport England.

When Ted died in 1998, a group of friends decided to celebrate his remarkable talent and contribution to Leisure Management by way of a book capturing his blend of wisdom and humour, distributed freely to those within and entering the field of leisure, sport and recreation management. This book of management insights is, however, not just a nostalgic celebration, but a means of passing on to a new generation of leisure managers and students the lessons of a great thinker and inspirational teacher.

In the late 1960s and early 1970s, a new profession of 'Recreation Management' was being born. Many in the emerging profession had knowledge and skills brought from careers in teaching, the forces and other disciplines, but it was Ted who opened our eyes to the fact that we were first and foremost MANagers (his emphasis, and with acknowledgement to political correctness – it was a while ago!), people who managed people, be they customers or staff.

One potential pitfall of recalling Ted in writing,

which we have tried to avoid, is to give Ted's ideas on management an academic interpretation, with the benefit of hindsight. We respect his uniqueness too much to try to analyse it. Ted is not easily presented in words on a page. We were captured and captivated by his ingenuity, the breadth of his knowledge, the depth of his understanding, and we understood that what he could do was beyond those of us who heard him, to recapture fully on paper. To understand Ted fully, you had to be there.

The other problem with trying to interpret Ted is that one of his greatest skills was to act as a synthesizer of general knowledge and management theory and to reinterpret it in a way which was relevant to leisure managers. Taking a management theory by Peter Drucker and making it accessible to a Trampolining coach, or presenting the psychology of Hertzberg in a way which could be understood by sports centre managers, was part of his skills. But, if you go looking for a 'Ted Blake Unified and Universal Theory of Management', you won't find it because it doesn't exist! Ted understood the importance of 'cut' and 'paste' a long time before Windows or 'Microsoft' Word!

But will the message of Ted Blake be relevant today? We were faced with the question: how do we get across the Man and the Message? We decided to use the qualities that Ted himself brought to his unique mission of management education: thorough research, humour, unexpectedness, visualisation and the entertainer's art of timing. Whether in politics or management, modern jargon cannot escape the 'sound bite'. However, this is not new. In terms of Leisure Management, Ted was probably the originator of the one-liner:

"If it can't be measured, it can't be managed"

"By the yard it's hard; by the inch, it's a cinch"

"If you think training costs are high, consider the cost of Ignorance!"

"There's no time like the pleasant".

Ted focused on leadership and the human factors of management – "mobilising people towards their full potential". He gave warnings about the traditional and rule-book approaches; he interpreted and adapted other writers and thinkers – "plagiarism is the most honest form of flattery", he would say. He quoted from philosophers and poets, "because I'm a Philistine and you lot also need a bit of culture".

Ted's words, humourous illustrations and unique style of delivery remain as relevant today as they were when he first expounded them. He was the Super Salesman – "Good salesmanship is NOT selling ice to Eskimos, but selling goods that don't come back to people who do"; "Helping people to make better decisions". He was the Great Communicator, Marketer, Motivator and Mentor, concerned with vision, values and core human needs, which he perceived as all-important in managing people, in successful selling and in business profitability. Ted

preached 'The Abundance Mentality' (as opposed to 'The Scarcity Mentality'), which he used in his 'Negotiating Skills' training sessions ... the Win/Win attitude.

He was never annoyed to find anyone using his material or "pinching his stuff", as his PA would call it. He'd say: "Well, it's not the only idea we'll ever have is it?"

In a personal reflection and recollection, one member of the Tribute Team (HG) recalled: "Like most of us, my first experience of Ted was hearing one of his inspirational lectures at some conference or seminar. Like most people, I was immediately captivated by his amazing ability to communicate, to put over radical and complex ideas in ways that made them seem simple. With a performer's slight of hand, he manipulated his audience with the same skill as he flipped, turned, passed and presented his fabulous overhead projector slides, leaving you in turn puzzled, bemused, entertained, enthralled, but invariably enlightened and usually laughing uproariously at some quip so clever, so apposite, but so bloody funny as well.

Everyone who was present at a Ted lecture, be it in a grand set piece conference or one of his local training seminars, is bound to recall some abiding image: the ugly old lady transformed into a beautiful girl to illustrate that things don't necessarily change, it's our (the customers') perceptions of them that is different as the point of view changes. He could tell us that the change depended on who you were, when you thought about it, how you started looking, or why you changed your position. The same illustration could illuminate a talk on the management of change or customer care. What made it interesting was the 'spin' (literally) that Ted put on it.

How many leisure managers went to hear Ted for a good laugh and ended up assimilating by osmosis the principles of the 'One Minute Manager' or Tom Peters' theories on service excellence?

But everyone has their favourite 'Tedism', usually an image remembered from a particularly vivid overhead slide. A particular favourite was the bumble bee. You will remember the picture – a large bulbous black and yellow insect, worried look on its face, its tiny wings beating frantically. Ted tells us completely seriously that scientists have proved irrefutably that, based on calculations of wingspan, wingspeed and power to weight ratio, it is impossible for the bumble bee ever to fly. "The trouble is" says Ted, swatting at an imaginary bee above his head, "nobody bothered to tell the bloody bumble bee", thus providing an opening into a dissertation about managerial inertia, or overcoming adversity, or the cross pollination of managerial ideas, or even the recent performances of Brentford Football Club!".

BOOK DESIGN AND CONTENT

Ted Blake left a legacy of written and visual materials in the form of published articles, occasional papers, conference and training course handouts, and, most importantly, hand-drawn, coloured overhead transparencies, which he used with wit and timing to delight his audiences. His humorous style, however, was targeted towards the achievement of excellence in management. At this point it is important to emphasise that this book contains only some of Ted's vast store of training ideas and materials, though they provide a taste and example of his genius.

As this publication is intended for a number of markets, from young students to experienced professionals, we have produced the book in a way which should have appeal 'across the board'. It is presented in two halves, theatrically, a 2-act play – Act 1 and Act 2!

<u>Act 1</u> sets the scene and includes what might be described as 'conventional' management. Scene I introduces the audience (the readers) to Ted's Management Skills, then moves to Scene II, Time Management; III, Leadership; IV, Delegation; V, Communication; VI, Staff Training and VII, Management by Objectives. The first part of the book eases the readers into the style of Blake, using all his own words and illustrations, but within the familiar language of conventional management, with some guidance and explanation.

In the Interval between the end of Act 1 and start of Act 2, a short summary is provided of the situation so far. By this stage, readers will have become familiar with the style of Ted Blake and the way in which he communicated his message. However, on stage Ted's delivery was at a rapid pace and an audience was bombarded with quick-fire illustrations and banter to drive home the points that he was making. Hence, to be true to Ted, the second half of the book, Act 2, adopts his delivery style, bombarding the senses with a succession of illustrations and anecdotes, but readers will by then be able to pick up the messages and tune into the subtle lessons and management insights.

<u>Act 2</u> starts with Ted's 'pièce de résistance' in scene one:

Scene i   Marketing;

Scene ii   Selling and Winning Customers;

Scene iii   Quality Customer Service;

Scene iv   The Art of Ted;

Scene v   Jokes, Quotes, Ted's favourite songs and poems;
and finally

The Curtain Call

Ted's
Manager and Management Skills

Most Management educators and trainers spend time on exploring what is meant by management. Ted Blake, never one to swim with the tide, did not dwell on 'management' per se. He focused on manager self-imaging and on management skills. In this first part of the book, Act 1, we focus on a mix of skills, including: Time Management; Leadership; Delegation; Communication; and Training. The essence of Ted's teaching, however, is captured in his philosophy, 'Become Your Own Hero – At Work' and what he called 'The Art of Lazy Management' – save yourself the effort!

Ted Blake was at his peak, in terms of leisure management, during the 1970s and 1980s, when the

'profession' of Leisure Management was in its infancy and only beginning to be recognised. He understood the need for those in the emerging profession to develop a positive self-image at a time when they were generally not given the respect as professional managers, particularly in local government, where many of the new leisure departments and leisure centres were being created. He set out to teach the profession that if it valued itself, then it would be valued in turn, and that a manager who is confident of his or her own abilities, will have the ability also to promote that confidence in the people who work with them and the people who use their facilities and services.

THE LAZY MANAGER!

Ted compares the effective Lazy Manager to the stressed, overworked, harassed Manager – are you in the office early

SELF CONCEPT:- I AM WHAT I SEE MYSELF TO BE

Harassed Manager

WHO is a Manager?

Anyone who is responsible....
(i.e. can make CHOICES about)

....for One, or More, other Persons

- ○ Work
- ○ Results } **You?**
- ○ Welfare

The Art of Lazy Management

i.e. Avoiding... just for a start...

- Waste of Time, Money, Effort etc
- Ambiguity of Purpose(s)
- Futility with Objectives
- Efficiency at Cost of Effectiveness
- Assumptive Communications
- Complicating Simple Processes
- Instant Gratifications
- Push, when Pull is better
- A "Scarcity" Mentality
- Delusions of Adequacy
  & more... so much more...

in the morning and late at night?

"Mummy, what is all that stuff in Daddy's briefcase?"

"It is work darling; they never give him enough time to finish it."

"Then why don't they put him in a slower class?"

Ted's message was, Lazy Managers work <u>SMARTER</u> – not Harder. SMART because S = Specific, M = Measurable, A = Attainable, R = Realistic and, most important, T = Time-bounded; exactly when it will end. They (not others) <u>start</u> with what <u>they</u> want to happen ...... where, when, why, how and by whom. He used Stephen Covey's, *The Seven Habits of Highly Effective People*, to demonstrate a 'Personal Effectiveness (Happenings) Plan'.

Management principles and ideas, which are sound, can last a lifetime. Ideas, in vogue today, such as 'empowerment'; 'enhancing value'; 'performance appraisal'; and 'self-assessment', were tackled by Ted Blake many years ago. For example, Ted linked his Art of Lazy Management to the concept of Empowerment – the 'facilitative' leader role – 'Set The People Free'. Delegate authority, not just work. Offer help without taking responsibility – so they can feel and claim "I or WE did it!"

Empowerment is seen as self-direction: *"Like an apple tree it does 3 things at once... people blossom; the whole job takes a nicer hue; and you get results."*

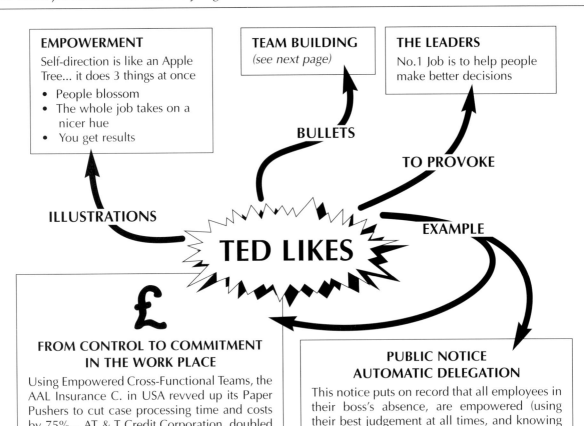

EMPOWERMENT
Self-direction is like an Apple Tree... it does 3 things at once
- People blossom
- The whole job takes on a nicer hue
- You get results

TEAM BUILDING
(see next page)

THE LEADERS
No.1 Job is to help people make better decisions

BULLETS

ILLUSTRATIONS

TO PROVOKE

TED LIKES

EXAMPLE

£

FROM CONTROL TO COMMITMENT IN THE WORK PLACE
Using Empowered Cross-Functional Teams, the AAL Insurance C. in USA revved up its Paper Pushers to cut case processing time and costs by 75%... AT & T Credit Corporation, doubled the number of lease applications processed each day... Goodyear Tyre Plant produces 50,000 tyres a day when comparable plants can only manage 25,000 per day... Semco in Brazil increased per employee productivity (Value Added) by 61%.

PUBLIC NOTICE AUTOMATIC DELEGATION
This notice puts on record that all employees in their boss's absence, are empowered (using their best judgement at all times, and knowing well that where they have choices they have responsibilities) to take all decisions, on all matters, in their own way, <u>except where otherwise agreed and recorded in writing</u>.

Dated
Managing Director

TEAM BUILDING

- We personally might be faster, cleverer, stronger; better in every way than any other single person in the team, but we cannot possibly be better than them all when they pull together.
- Bosses, colleagues, subordinates are our INTERNAL customers – Treat 'em as such.
- Remember ... throwing a colleague an 11ft rope when he's drowning 20 ft away is not more than meeting him half way. Go the whole way.
- Communication is the glue that binds teams together. Keep them all informed... early... fully... sensitively.
- Wherever possible communicate verbally and personally. The function of most memos is not to help the recipient but to cover our own backside. There has to be a better way to achieve both.
- Token jobs – spending a day working in an associated department can do wonders for understanding their problems and needs and prevent department warfare.
- Cooperation is vital. Conflict dealt with in a constructive way, can actually strengthen cooperation. Don't stifle creativity. Listen to all suggestions. Remember, an idea doesn't care who had it.
- Don't shift the blame or apologise to customers for other people or departments and don't make promises without checking that they can/will deliver.
- Don't knock other departments. Concentrate on WHAT is wrong rather than who is wrong. Separate the problem from the people.
- N-E-T-M-A (Nobody Ever Tells Me Anything) As a manager or supervisor, make sure your team gets the information from you, not through the grapevine or from another source.

Ted Blake's guides to 'Empowerment' and 'Employee Performance Appraisal', pages 14–16, going back to 1972, illustrates his far-sightedness.

EMPOWERMENT IS.....

- a   guarantee of FULL EMPLOYMENT ....of those **with** jobs
- the most productive technology since the Industrial Revolution
- the most liberating organisational change since the French Revolution
- true scientific management i.e. exploration of the future by questions, hypothesis, testing and prediction
- a true innovation of Creative Destruction and Planned Obsolescence
- each person holding a FRANCHISE on their jobs; prescriptions to grant self managed team work; privileges and exemption in accordance with objectives
- the death of paternalistic hierarchy and birth of Multiple Team Formation
- facilitative leadership, enabling staff to use best judgements about the How, Where and When of Process, without managers losing the authority to decide the Why and What content i.e. there is no anarchy, abdication or loss of authority
- PRO ACTIVE management i.e. TELLING them Why, but ASKING them How
- BREEDING "Intrapreneurs", taking initiatives that nobody before would have thought of asking them to take, with managers deferring urges to say 'Yes But...'
- asking for, and giving help, without taking away responsibility
- managers becoming First Assistants to their subordinates
- meeting people's needs, not for power, but to achieve something and be somebody
- using sequentially, Awareness..... Understanding..... Competence..... and Commitment to create never-ending improvements
- exploiting the most under-used form of remuneration; Significance, Creativity, Building your own Security. If it cannot be measured, can it ever be managed?
- redirecting all the energies in beating the system into transforming the systems
- surrendering the convention that Managers do the Thinking, Supervisors do the Talking, and Staff do the Doing. Success or failure do not exist except by Arbitrary definition.
- probably the best way ever to retain and develop your best people, i.e Capital Appreciation and Investment in People
- NOT Power Sharing... a Zero Sum where if one gets more, the others must get less. Its Power GENERATION - the avoidance of negative expectations
- fostering the Abundance Mentality, NEW Power Creation, via Win/Win Negotiation... Conflict without Confrontation, Confidence not Conformity

- Less Domination by Telling and Finger Wagging; but more Power to BOTH sides by Asking
- NOT laissez faire or Management by Exception; it's fast automatic trust and action
- NOT Teaching but Learning; not correction but coaching, emphasising what people ARE
- NOT judging staff's intentions and capabilities by management's fears
- Rethinking all the old ways, creating and learning new ways, i.e. 'Aha' Experiences
- NOT 'Charismatic' leadership... Golden Eggs are laid by the Geese, not Peacocks
- The end or salvation of Middle Management.... those mediating hurdles or bridges between supplicants and higher authority who now have the greatest opportunities for change

Self-direction applies to the work of individuals and teams. Ted compared Self-directed teams to Traditional departments.

DRAMATIC RESULTS

Traditional departments	Self-directed teams
Take directions	Take initiatives
Seek individual rewards	Focus on team contributors
Focus on blame	Concentrate on solutions
Compete	Co-operate
Stop at pre-set goals	Continually improve
Demand more resources	Work with what they have
React to emergencies	Take steps to prevent emergencies
Spend money	Save money
TO improve quality	BY improving quality

Guide to Employee Performance Appraisal

FACTORS	Far exceeds job requirement	Exceeds job requirement	Meets job requirement	Needs improvement	Below minimum requirement
Communication	Talks with god	Talks with angels	Talks to himself	Argues with himself	Sulks when he loses these arguments
Adaptability	Walks on water constantly	Walks on water in emergencies	Washes hand with water in emergencies	Exudes water in emergencies	Passes water in emergencies
Drive	Leaps tall building with a single bound	Needs a run up to leap over tall buildings	Can leap over short buildings only	Crashes into buildings when trying to leap over them	Cannot recognise a building of any sort
Impact	Reminds you of Napoleon	Reminds you of Josephine	Could be your son but then you are married	Psycho ceramic or a crack pot	A case of mistaken identity
Attitude to Errors	Can be outspoken but nobody hears	Shows great creativity in rationalisation	Forges his way through them	Generous to a fault he delegates it	Has many faults but being wrong isn't one of them
Cooperation	Blessed are the meek for they shall inhibit the earth	Gives too freely of what he needs himself e.g. advice	Believes all should share work, especially those with jobs	Has a chip on both shoulders but it doesn't help his balance	Always does it the herd way
Hobbies	Mountain climbing over mole hills	Kite flying and string pulling	Trying to get ahead to replace the one he has	Crossing asparagus with mustard to get hot tips	Feeding the birds to dogs, cats etc.
Sensitivity	Rides horses backwards. Knows looking over their shoulder makes them nervous	Keeps friends because he never gives them away	Quietly calm and strong as an ox. Almost as clever	Hasn't got an enemy in the world, but all his friends hate him	Dull but steady. Would make a good parent
Experience	20 years in identical one year packets	Not exaggerated just remember big	Regards it as a comb for a bald headed man	Every company is after him – Gas Company, Finance Company	A disgrace to self and former employers but then they did try

ACTIONS THAT SEPARATE CUSTOMER
FOCUS
WINNERS FROM STRUGGLING COMPANIES

STRUGGLING COMPANIES	CUSTOMER FOCUS WINNERS
Distracted managers and employees seek business opportunities everywhere **HEADLESS CHICKENS**	Managers and employees focus laser-like on being the best in the world at providing value for well-defined, targeted customers
Companies invest heavily in poorly coordinated customer research and take little action on the data! **WE MUST FIRST GET THE FACTS!?**	Companies develop clear listening strategies and then hardwire what they learn into the company so employees predictably deliver what customers seek
Fashionable trends like "total quality" have disrupted ways of work, but no consistent new way of getting things done has emerged! **WHO ACCREDITS QUALITY?**	Shared superordinate goals, wise investments in training, and a well designed infrastructure produce a collaborative way of working that's **visible** everywhere
Salespeople pressured to maximise orders; service is a support function treated as a necessary evil! **IS IT WHAT WE SELL? OR WHAT WE BUY?**	The Company develops a proprietary customer interaction process that is as much a part of what its brand stands for as the core product itself
Executives try to reposition their companies by force of their own decisions or to 'go back to basics' when the basics don't work anymore! i.e. **BE REMOTE, SEPARATED, TELL AND CONTROL**	Contract leadership emerges as managers come out of their ivory towers to customer work sites and to places in the organisation where real work gets done!

Adapted by Ted Blake from 'Customer Centered Growth' by Whitely and Hessan
Published by Random House 1996. (Century Business) ISBN 0 7126 7712 7
Ted Blake liked to interpret and adapt other people's ideas
– Can you Spot the Ted Additions to the Table. Plagiarism is the most honest form of flattery!!

"Kiss" is the Key to Clarity...

<u>K</u>eep <u>I</u>t <u>S</u>imple – <u>S</u>tupid!

and please forgive long letter.....just not enough time to make it a short one

Are YOU here with the Solution ... or are <u>you</u> part of the <u>Problem</u>?

14ft high. Cut from one flawed block of marble.

1504

The <u>David</u> Solution
"Tell us Michelangelo, how you created this masterpiece statue of David in 3 Years?"
"It's easy. You just chip away the bits that... Don't Look Like David."

BLAKE

Be careful of ending up with other people's monkeys to care for!

Ted believed in recreation

Ted recognised recreation had to fight for its slice.

Perception of Facts

In Leningrad...
..Freezing Point

is called

Melting Point

ANTONIO STRADIVARI   1644 - 1737
Characteristic bridge, shallow body, varnish which is still a secret and set proportions for all modern violins.

Customer Care

"Platform 15—you'll just catch it...if you run..."

BLAKE

Ted on Time Management

The resources available to management are usually thought of as 'people, money and materials'. But there is another unique resource – time. You can't buy it, save it or stop it. It cannot be stored; it is irreplaceable; once spent it is gone. Leisure managers will be acutely aware of time's perishability, dealing as they do with the theatre seat or tennis court, not sold today, being lost forever. The efficient use of a manager's time is crucially important in achieving aims and objectives, getting priorities right, meeting deadlines and coping with work overload, stress and strain. As Ted Blake said:

"If you can't manage your own time... you certainly can't manage anybody else's."

We all have the same amount of time – good managers and poor managers. Good managers find the most relevant and powerful ways of employing time:

It is not time that is scarce
It is our management of it.

> **How Many People, on Their Deathbeds, Wish They'd Spent More Time at the Office?**

THE 20/80 PRINCIPLE

Ted Blake preached a gospel of 'be aware of just how valuable your time is for business; resolve not to waste it'. He quoted often: "Don't work harder – work smarter" using the Italian economist, Wilfredo Pareto's 20/80 principle – 20% effort produces 80% effect; 20% of

REALITY?

See page 120 for solution

our jobs produce 80% of income and so on. When applied to time, it states 20% of our time determines 80% of our performance.

STRESS AND STRAIN

Ted had a lot to say about stress and strain – a pre-occupation today of many psychologists and 'stress consultants'. Contrary to popular belief, our productivity – our effectiveness – increases with stress, to be 'fired up' to achieve – to do our job. But stress is needed only to a critical point. Beyond that point, greater stress becomes counterproductive. It becomes strain. Ted Blake clarifies:

"In metallurgy, a distinction is made between stress and strain. Strain occurs when a metal is taken beyond its elastic limit, the inference being that stress is not really harmful .... It can be quite productive. But once the flexibility of a person (elastic limit) has been reached, you are going to get strain".

Stress beyond the critical point, reflects a failure to cope with certain situations and is induced, in large measure, by:

• Poor management of time
• Attempting too much
• Trying to concentrate on too many things at the same time
• Lack of planning
• Procrastination
• Worry

- Concentrating on activities rather than objectives and
- Crisis management

Therefore, Ted would advocate: Plan; Set Objectives; Choose Priorities; and Stick to them (unless emergency occurs). He would use phrases, such as: 'Avoid the tyranny of the (seemingly) urgent. Concentrate on the important'. And Ted is right: we are bombarded daily with unimportant, seemingly urgent, calls, emails, mobile phone text messages and faxes!

CRISIS MANAGEMENT

Probably the greatest failing of managers (all of us) is leaving important jobs till the last minute, then working like mad to get them done! The term Crisis Management comes to mind and Ted would probably agree with Murphy's Laws: "Nothing is as simple as it seems. Everything takes longer than you think. If anything can go wrong, it will."

A few managers appear to flourish in a perpetual state of crisis, theatrically barking out orders, demanding instant action, getting things done, making money. But, in general, it is the unsuccessful managers who jolt from crisis to crisis, unable to handle situations.

PROCRASTINATION!

Emotionally, we tend to do the things we like to do. However, putting things off not only stops us getting things done, it builds up workload, pressure and worry and loses opportunities. Putting things off – procrastination – is not laziness. Often, the procrastinator works unsparingly on other things which he or she likes to do better. Ted Blake once said that some leisure directors have taken so long to address problems, that they find excuses to get someone else involved to solve them!

The time management message from Ted Blake is uncomplicated:

- Schedule the important, the difficult, the unpleasant tasks first, second and third.
- Stop the hidden prevarication of 'clearing the decks to get down to it'.
- Follow Ted's 'little and often' maxim: "Inch by inch, it's a cinch. Yard by yard, it's hard".
- Delegate; get others to share.
- Set deadlines; go public.
- Set standards, but don't demand impossible perfection.
- Don't say yes to unreasonable requests; don't shoulder everyone's problems.

Ted's over-riding message in this context is:

CONCENTRATE ON THE PRIORITIES – THE PRODUCTIVE FEW.

Ted on
Leadership

Lives of great men all remind us
We can make our lives sublime
And, departing, leave behind us
Footprints on the Sands of Time
  [Longfellow, often quoted by Ted Blake].

Good management is largely the result of good managers, individuals who have the responsibility for providing leadership of the organisation and the ability to move it towards its goals.

Of the three core elements of skill needed by the manager – conceptual, human and technical –

Abraham Lincoln talking to General George Meade on the eve prior to the battle of Gettysburg – July 1-3 1863

"Few of our soldiers would sell us their lives for a million dollars....yet most will willingly give us their lives for a flag & a bit of ribbon. Do we have enough flags & ribbon?"

Ted Blake concentrated on the human factors. Good leadership requires an understanding of people and their distinctiveness, humorously depicted in the cartoon on 'Differences'! – ourselves, colleagues and customers.

People don't want what Leadership IS.. (..stylish or otherwise.)
NEWS
They Want what Leadership Does.
Give 'em frequent Positive Feedback ...
..it Rewards-Informs-Clarifies Satisfies-Sets Standards-Kills Negativism
It needs to: Get Attention-Be Immediate-Name Names-Be Varied & Accurate
NEWS

Why do Symbols feature so importantly in All our lives? Because they guarantee that most desired of All emotional needs...

... **INSTANT RESPECT**

⚖️ **BLAKE**

Ted wrote:

"Leadership is the influence an individual exerts over a group. The people who are to be led determine the nature and qualifications of the leader. Leadership is neither good nor bad except in the group context .... Other theories include:

- *Facilitative leadership that informs, enables and empowers others to assume situational leaderships appropriate to burgeoning abilities.*
- *Coaching leadership, where the leader is content to point the way, but by using questions instead of statements followers discover, and therefore own, truths and skills – education (E in Latin = Out; duco = I lead). <u>Don't forget, values are caught rather than taught.</u>*
- *Military leadership – a contradiction in terms.*
- *Manipulative leadership, or Divide and Rule.*
- *Charismatic leadership that is the apparent effectiveness or peacocking (geese lay the golden eggs, not peacocks) and*
- *One-eyed Man King Among the Blind, or Witch Doctor Leadership, the sapiential style beloved by experts and consultants."*

[Blake in <u>Recreation</u>, March 1994]

Leadership cannot be separated from management, though management is not leadership, per se. An unorganised group can have a leader, but managers only exist in an organised structure where specific roles have been created. As Ted said, you

don't need to be a manager to be a leader but you'll never be a real manager unless you're a leader.

"Managers are appointed. Leaders are chosen."

Leadership has been described as a mixture of art, craft and humanity. It is an essential part of a manager's job. A good leader is concerned both with people and results. Leadership is a word with positive connotations. We look to leaders to inspire, direct and pave the way. In leisure management, there is a need for excellent leaders at all levels.

Ted Blake used the words 'Management' and 'Leadership' in his own way and sometimes was challenged for doing so.

In the illustration *'Management vs Leadership'* Ted appeared to denigrate management in favour of leadership, but in a subsequent article he explained more fully what he was getting at.

MANAGEMENT	LEADERSHIP
Authority is invested in the POSITION	Authority is invested in the PERSON
Is all about Stability	Is all about Change
Is about Compliance	Is about Commitment
Is about Means	Is about Ends
Is Efficient	Is Effective
Does Things Right	Does Right Things
Is a Map	Is a Compass
Is How	Is Why
Responds	Pre-empts
Meeting Objectives	Clarifying Values
Is more of a Science	Is more of an Art
Usually likes to Tell	Usually likes to Ask
Form follows the Function	Form determines Function

"Some readers have complained that my articles imply that leadership is better than management. It isn't. It is just less common.

There is no conflict between leadership and management. They are complementary, not competitive, each stronger or weaker with, or without, the other. Each has its place, its time, its purpose and processes, as appropriate. For example, inventors lead conceptually by dreaming up new ideas which, although they may be brilliant, could come to nothing unless actualised by good management.... Without leadership, few outstanding ideas appear. Without good management, they quickly disappear."

[Blake in <u>Recreation</u>, September 1994].

Ted believed that some managers at all levels, including the top level, are poor leaders. Some so-called 'leaders', he said, really need to be called 'administrators'! Generally, in leisure, a highly visible 'profession', managers without good leadership qualities cannot be said to be good managers. Ted's philosophy – 'Managers double their influence with Leadership' – would mirror the management guru, Peter Drucker's, insight: 'As a leader, you are visible; incredibly visible. And you have expectations to fulfil'.

A strong perception of leadership, handed down through the ages, is that of the generals leading the troops into battle. Leadership, fortunately, covers far wider territories than waving a flag and drumming a drum. There are other angles to leadership. Managerial leadership skills are not always overtly discernible. We can evidence this with some conductors of an orchestra or with captains in sport, who

most organisations. Leadership moves the organisation along the chosen route towards its goals. Leadership provides the drive and the direction.

Unlike good leadership, which may be difficult to define, poor leadership exhibits a wide range of easily recognisable traits in a person: insensitivity to others, overbearing, over supervising, failing to delegate, seeking praise first instead of giving praise to colleagues, blaming, finding scapegoats, indecision and so on.

Good leaders must have the ability to inspire followers through the use of appeal and persuasion. Ted Blake certainly inspired a generation of leisure, sport and recreation professionals – to respect themselves and to make us all feel 10ft. tall!

quietly get the best out of their players without shouting from the rooftops. (For cricket enthusiasts, recall Mike Brearley's captaincy of 'Beefy' – Ian Botham). Ted's message was that managers are not here to command, but to <u>convince</u>, and so get consent, depicted colourfully in the illustration, 'In the Next Decade ...'.

Leaders, then, need to: direct; support; inspire; and communicate. Leadership is closely associated with directing – clearly informing people what, when and how to do a job and then supervising performance. In the management situation, leadership could be said to be 'people power' – the powerhouse of

MOTIVATION

Many people involved in leisure need very little motivation. Leisure managers, trainees, sports and arts teachers and coaches, countryside rangers, music directors, museum curators, play leaders, tourism managers and holiday activity organisers, in the main, are highly motivated to begin with. This gives leisure leadership a head start, Ted would say, over selling used cars and double glazing.

However, there is a responsibility, Ted would argue, for an organisation to develop its staff and motivate them through more challenging areas of responsibility and experience. This will give employees the opportunity to achieve a greater self-worth in the job, while the organisation will benefit through having a more productive and flexible workforce.

Staff need to work at their potential. If they do not, they can be an expensive liability to the organisation and they weaken the team. A motivated workforce is more likely to be successful than a de-motivated team. Pulling together is better than pulling apart. And here Ted would use the analogy of the proficient tug-of-war team. When people work as a team, they motivate each other – no-one wants to let the side down – and as a result, the team is more productive. Staff will **feel**, **think** and **work** like a team.

DIFFERENT STYLES OF LEADERSHIP
– Use More Than One Club!

Different managers have different styles of leadership. The same manager may also have a number of different styles, depending on the different situations. A manager armed with only one style, will be ill-equipped for the different tasks and people to be handled – just like the golfer with only one club, says Ted. The brilliant cartoon of the pirate ship shows dramatically the ultimate autocratic style! *(shown later in full colour)*

The business of leisure, where people choose what to do, and where staff have to be flexible and work unsocial hours, calls for styles of management in keeping with providing good customer service and also care of staff.

Different styles of leadership will be appropriate to different situations. Ted, who revealed the importance of employee involvement and participation in decision-making, says:

"If you are going to bark every time you stand up, people will soon fail to listen".

The inimitable Ted, in his illustration, 'What's Your Style', portrays more-effective managers and contrasts them with less-effective managers:

WHAT'S YOUR STYLE!?

Missionary   "Has a speech impediment – can't say no to Anybody!"

Compromiser   "Gives everybody a definite 'maybe'; he is the best of the worst – not bad enough to fire, yet not good enough to keep!"

Autocrat   "Says, Teamwork is a lot of people doing what I say."

Deserter   "When the crap hits the fan, the deserter is probably the cause of it and will then probably sue you under the HASAWA!"

Ted Blake provided an interesting matrix of 18 situations under 4 styles of leadership which he called: 'Separated' (Enough Only); 'Related' (People First); 'Dedicated' (Job First); and the best 'Integrated' (Job Through People).

COACH AND MENTOR

Coaching is not just an activity on the sports ground. Staff in organisations need good coaches to bring out the best from them.

A leisure management 'coach' can also be a 'mentor' [a term taken from Homer's Odyssey. Ted would say, "Let's bring a little culture to you Philistines"]. Visionary leaders make good mentors because they have principles and values which stem from inner convictions. As Ted's skeleton runner cartoon depicts: principles last; practices don't. These convictions, enthusiastically projected, influence others positively. They have trodden the path before; they can empathise.

A mentor is an experienced guide, promoting the cause and showing the way – a teacher and coach who can make a lasting impression on an individual's life. College students will know the value of an inspiring personal tutor. Mentors provide a helping hand, inspire mutual trust, loyalty and friendship.

PRINCIPLES LAST.
PRACTICES DON'T

YESTERDAY

enthusiastically supported by Ted. It is based on the needs of people. The object is that the service given to them enables them to grow into healthier, wiser and more fulfilled people and contributing citizens. [Read *Inner Quest* from The Greenleaf Centre for Servant – Leadership]

A lasting impression of Ted Blake is that he saw leadership as getting excellent results, through a team of people who make the best decisions they can in any given situation, and who feel good about themselves and their work.

Professions such as law and accountancy include a time when graduates must work with qualified professionals to 'learn the ropes'. In this process, the 'apprentice' absorbs an approach, a style, a life view, which can shape their future. Ted Blake believed we needed much more coaching and mentoring in leisure management.

SERVANT LEADERSHIP

For people to benefit from leisure, other people have to give service. The recent concept, that of the 'servant-leader' – caring leadership – fits well into many aspects of the profession of leisure management and would, most likely, have been

SUCH
SELF-IMAGING
CAN BECOME A
POWERFUL REALITY

AS A MANAGER
BE YOUR
OWN HERO
AT WORK

BLAKE

Ted on
Delegation

A saying goes: "Don't put off until tomorrow that which you can get someone else to do today."

Managers are responsible for more than they can achieve by their own efforts. Delegation is the work a manager has to have undertaken, but entrusts and gives authority to others to undertake it and get the results. A delegate, then, is a person authorised to act as a representative for another or others. But, as Ted Blake warned, a manager can delegate authority, but not ultimate responsibility.

Ted is clear as to what is and what is not delegation:

The boss may continue to do the job he has just left; it's easier than his new one, and he liked the old.

So here I am delegating

I've given him a job and now I'm doing it with or for him. WHY? Because its a bloody sight easier than the 20% I should be getting on with.

"If what you are 'delegating' is not part of your job, then it isn't delegation, it is merely organisation".

So, don't 'delegate' simple tasks, mundane work you haven't got time for or don't like to do. This can be patronising and demoralising. Delegating is not simply off-loading tasks and 'buck-passing'. And don't carry on doing the job you have already 'delegated', as depicted in the Boss cartoon!

Don't have employees following orders – give them a mission to accomplish.

Recall Parkinson's Law, Ted would say, which shows the need to stretch staff, otherwise 'work tends to expand to fill the time available for its completion'.

However, there are some areas of work that should never be delegated, such as highly confidential matters, disciplining, and areas in which only the delegator has the power.

Thus, delegation for a leisure manager, Ted explains, can free up time for key priorities and build up competences of staff and enhance their professional growth and development. It also allows decisions to be taken at the appropriate level and

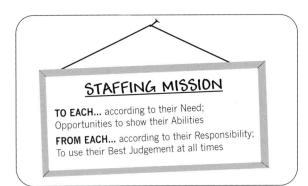

STAFFING MISSION

TO EACH... according to their Need; Opportunities to show their Abilities

FROM EACH... according to their Responsibility; To use their Best Judgement at all times

increases effectiveness. However, there is need for delegation clarity: focus attention on the results and standards; and be concise about the power being handed on.

In *The Seven Habits of Highly Effective People* [A book highly commended by Ted Blake], Stephen Covey differentiates between 'gofer delegation' and 'stewardship delegation'. Gofer delegation means, "Go for this, go for that, do this, do that, and tell me when it's done". It spawns a creed which says: "Tell me what you want me to do, and I'll do it".

Stewardship delegation is focused on results instead of methods. It involves mutual commitment to expectations – what, not how; results, not methods.

Two key messages come from Ted in this context:

Time spent training someone to do a job is repaid many times over,
and
Do nothing you can, and should, delegate.

Delegating...

... is <u>not</u>
   giving others <u>work to do</u>...

... but
   <u>results and goals to Achieve</u>!

 BLAKE

Ted on
Communication

Excellent communication is an essential component of good management. Communicating is not just verbal and written, but also has to do with the manner of the communication. "I understand" may be received as "I hear and disagree and will not change my opinion" and, one real giveaway, is "I hear you", i.e. your words are heard and instantly dismissed. Hence, atmosphere – you could have cut the air with a knife

**"Who else do you
want to humiliate
this morning?"**

– facial expressions, the movement of the eyes, and sitting positions, whether made consciously or unconsciously, can all convey much to the receiver of the sender's attitude and vice-versa.

One-way communication is quick, often satisfying for the sender, but more often frustrating for the receiver and it can lead to misunderstanding. Two-way communication takes longer, it is more sensitive and more accurate. To communicate, we must understand others. Each one of us is different from everyone else.

has been another futile pastime of mine. Now, if letters, memos, etc. put forward ideas with which I cannot possibly agree, I just write back ...

..."There's a great deal in what you say Jim ...."

No need to say a great deal of what, they are sure to take it the right way. If they were not looking for approval, they would not put the ideas forward and we all tend to see what we want to see. If you write to me after this talk ... *"There's a great deal in what you said Ted."* I can't misunderstand you."

Ted was a great communicator. His slogan was **A.I.D.A.** He never failed to gain our **'Attention'**, hold our **'Interest'**, and stimulate a **'Desire'** to instigate an **'Action'**. He said:

Effective communication needs to be built upon an understanding of people. Ted's analysis was:

"Every person is like .....

All other people

Some other people

No other person
Identifying in which respect helps Communication".

Ted points out his shortcoming when writing to some people!

"Writing to tell people they are wrong ...

"Communication is the initiation, transmission and sharing of information, meanings, understandings, conclusions, decisions and responses. It is never the message sent out that counts – only the message received. By definition all effective communication has to be self-serving, to produce for the communicator a specific outcome or effect. Like murder, there is always MOM – motive, an opportunity and a means.

The purpose, i.e. the why of communication is to contact, measure, maintain, or change, i.e. to influence others. This influence "derives much, if not most of, its strength from being secret" (Michael Shea, former Press Secretary to the Queen)."

[Blake in <u>Recreation</u>, April 1997]

A high-risk strategy used by Ted Blake seemed to work for him as in his letter to "Dear Jim". [We should add 'use with caution'!].

Ted enlivened the process by the fun and humour underlying the promotion of his ideas. However, he used many techniques and just for the fun of it (as Ted might say) assess your own

TBI (Ted Blake Index – *see following page*). Ted would probably have scored close to 10/10!

TBI 10 POINT PLAN

Ted Blake distinguishes the processes of 'Communication' and 'Presentation', ending on a salutary note, and one that sums up his message on communication:

***"It's never the message sent out that counts .....
only the one Received!"***

	Communication	**Presentation**
Levels	Data	Emotion
Question	What – Who – Why	How – Where – When
Aims	Logic, to inform	Respect, to influence
Values	"Goodness"	Rightness
Leads to	Conclusions	Decisions
Relies on	Facts	Judgements
Joint Purpose	**To change, or maintain, the 3 A's...** **A**wareness – **A**ttitude – **A**ction	
Sequence	(Open) (Middle) (Close)	
Golden Rule	<u>**First**</u> seek to understand... in order to be better understood	
Personal Motives	To dominate – Make statements To control – Ask questions	
Measure	Always – Always get feedback	
Last Thoughts	It's never the message sent out that counts... only the one **Received!**	

TBI 10 POINT PLAN

Do you:

1 <u>Know your audience</u>
   Invariably Ted would identify with his audience by referring to 'figureheads' that were present.

2 <u>Research your subject</u>
   Ted possessed an extensive library and used facts, figures, graphs, quotations to good effect.

3 <u>Rehearse your presentation</u>
   Ted and Jean Mackenzie were as professional as Paul Daniels and Debbie McGhee.

4 <u>Optimise the use of audio/visual/electronic technology</u>
   Ted used his hand-drawn overheads as an integral part of his presentation, and music for a 'wake-up' start and a memorable, emotional finish.

5 <u>Explain – summarise – develop your message with a hand-out</u>
   Most of the current leaders in leisure management will have a 'Ted Blake folder', somewhere in their office or home.

6 <u>Package your thoughts in easily remembered acronyms</u>
   Can anyone forget the 'S.W.O.T'? analysis and 'KISS' principle?

7 <u>Highlight your bullet points and use the humourous cartoon</u>
   Ted was a gifted illustrator and skillfully used his artistic talents.

8 <u>Use the humourous one-liner</u>
   Ted (the original 'soundbite' creator for leisure management) realised that the average person recalls 30% more when humour is used to inform and instruct.

9 <u>Use 'colour' in your illustrations</u>
   Ted used his reds, greens and blues. Take a look at two of his illustrations on the next pages.

10 <u>Keep your audience smiling</u>
   Ted did, and was always asked back for more.

<u>Strictly Private and Confidential</u>

2/12/95

Dear Jim

Please forgive handwritten note but, as you can see from the attached, some <u>NUT</u> is using your notepaper & forging your respected signature to try & promote ill-will between us.

He might have succeeded but his clear ignorance of our high regard for you & your reputation for fairness betrayed him of course. I will keep this confidential & it might be prudent to destroy these items as in the wrong hands they could do untold harm etc.

Ted on
Training

Training said Ted *"is like parachute jumping... you have got to get it right first time!"*

In demonstrating his philosophy of teaching and training, Ted often quoted 'Paracelsus' by Robert Browning ...

> *"To know consists in opening out a way whence the inner splendour can escape,*
> *Rather than effecting entrance for a light supposed to be without."*

Leisure is a growth industry of national significance in social and economic terms. Employment on this scale raises substantial questions about training and career development in the profession of leisure, sports, arts and recreation management. Without qualified and trained staff at all levels, no leisure business or service can hope to be effective.

The training market is large: people employed in the leisure industry – public, commercial and voluntary sectors; people in related professions such as education and community work; and people seeking employment in the industry.

Ted Blake began to write and lecture about training in 'Recreation Management' before UK universities and colleges established academic studies and qualifications in the subject. But Ted didn't follow the traditional

Give a man some fish... and he can eat for a day.

Teach him HOW to fish... and he can eat for the rest of his life.

The cost of Ignorance ...can be a Lifetime of Dependence.

One days training can be worth so very much more than one days fish... or wages...if appropriate to your need

Ancient Chinese Proverb

I hear it . . . . . and I forget

I see it . . . . . . and I remember

I do it . . . . and I <u>Know</u>

"and to know . . . .
consists of opening up a way whence the inner splendour may escape . . . rather than trying to effect entry for a light supposed to be without"

from "Paracelsus" by Robert Browning

> Training is the Boss's
> Nº I responsibility
> to his subordinates
>
> Managing Director
> OR?
> Chief Training Officer
> I'm called one and do the other

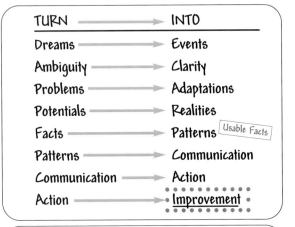

Any of your ideas ...
... you can get
← "THEM" to "discover"...

... helps prove that
Managers are not there to
lean on ... but to make any
leaning unnecessary.

education may be seen as a process of learning and enquiry, with learner input a part of the process. Management training may be seen as an input process from teacher to learner, whereby the learner is equipped with job-related knowledge and skills for job success. Management development may be seen as increasing the manager's adaptability and flexibility, maximising strengths and overcoming weaknesses.

TURN	→	INTO
Dreams	→	Events
Ambiguity	→	Clarity
Problems	→	Adaptations
Potentials	→	Realities
Facts	→	Patterns Usable Facts
Patterns	→	Communication
Communication	→	Action
Action	→	Improvement

Check your Subordinates'
Outputs irregularly...

... Aim to Catch 'em doing

Something RIGHT!

It's impossible to be on Good Terms with
anything ... unless you are on good terms with Yourself.
Goals begin Behaviours,
Consequences maintain 'em

and academic routes, though he wasn't anti-education; indeed, as a trained, gifted and highly qualified teacher and educationalist, he valued education in the broadest sense; today, he would certainly be an advocate of 'Life Long Learning'. However, in terms of management, Ted was a staunch proponent of training. It is not surprising, therefore, that Ted ended his outstanding professional career as a sought-after Management Trainer for a number of different professions.

The terms management 'training', 'education' and 'development' are often used interchangeably or one term will encompass the three. Management

 BLAKE

There are also schools of thought about training: leisure and recreation are separate from management and can be taught apart; leisure and recreation management is an area in its own right, with a set of specialist skills; and leisure management is composed of subdivisions such as sports management, arts management and so on.

Ted did not get too tied up with this debate, though, even as a strong advocate of training, he also came to the conclusion –

"no training can put in what God left out".

HEALTH AND SAFETY AT WORK

As the Managing Director of a highly successful manufacturing and production company, Ted Blake was acutely aware of the training that was needed for all in terms of safety, and the human and legal

consequences of poor safety training. As Ted says in the illustrations, "Safety is NO accident .... It is the Best Design". We should assume that everyone is 'an idiot' and be a stickler for the procedures and documentation.

It is impossible to make everything
IDIOT PROOF...

... as Idiots are so Ingenious but a good training
programme that assumes that everybody is an idiot...
at something... will enable you
to keep up... if never ahead

No single *Snowflake* ever feels responsible for an Avalanche

STANDARDS AND QUALIFICATIONS

In recent times in the UK, significant change has come about with the introduction of National Vocational Qualifications (NVQs & SNVQs in Scotland), Industry Lead Bodies (ILBs) and National Training Organisations (NTOs). Ted Blake would be pleased that NTOs are employer-led initiatives, and NVQs based on Competence Standards.

SkillsactiveUK (formerly SPRITO) is the NTO which covers the wide field of leisure, recreation, sport and play and is heavily involved in establishing clear entry and career progression routes into the industry. It is also concerned with Best Practice in support of continuous improvement in the workplace.

A quality scheme called QUEST was designed as the Business Excellence Model for the industry; clear links with the government's Best Value culture is evident. It is of interest that, many years ago, Ted Blake was advocating and lecturing on the European Business Excellence Model, now used as the UK model. The QUEST Self-assessment Quality approach is based on the Business Excellence Model.

And what of the future? The Hospitality Industry has already launched training and education electronically – a University on the Internet. Never one to miss a challenge, we wonder what Ted Blake would have made of that – a training 'cop-out' or great opportunity!?

VALUES AND CREDIBILITY

Ted Blake's teaching and ethos is summed up in Einstein's words:

"Train .... not to be a man of Success, but a man of Value. Then .... you are a man of Success!"

Ted concludes: "The only real authority you have got is your credibility .... and Training can give you that". His message is clear:

Train 'em Systematically ... or every time they have a Tea Break... you may find it necessary to Re-Train 'em

"Good Morning, Judge".

... and if there ever is a CASE... you will probably find it LOST or WON... ... on One Thing Alone...

Check List

Documentation

Inspire and motivate people and train them in the essential manager and management skills – this will lead to success.

Einstein

"Train...
..not to be a man of Success but a man of Value.
Then...
..you ARE a man of Success!"

The only real authority you have got is your credibility...
and Training can give you that

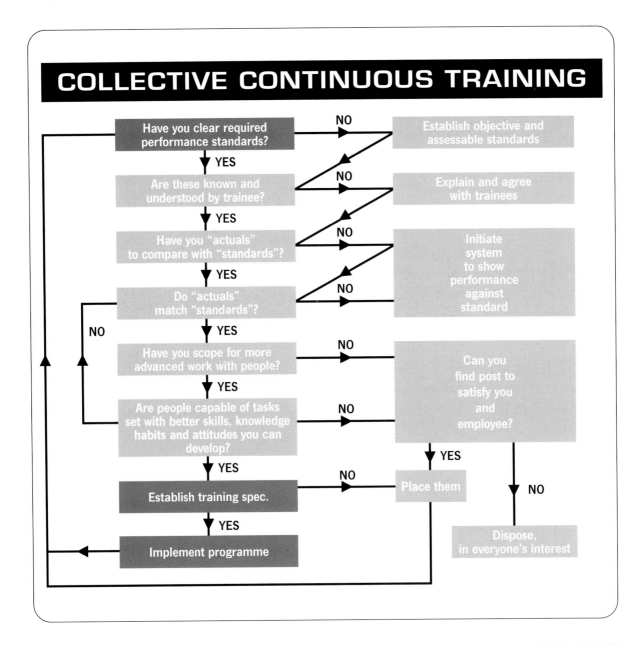

COLLECTIVE CONTINUOUS TRAINING

Have you clear required performance standards? — NO → **Establish objective and assessable standards**

↓ YES

Are these known and understood by trainee? — NO → **Explain and agree with trainees**

↓ YES

Have you "actuals" to compare with "standards"? — NO → **Initiate system to show performance against standard**

↓ YES

Do "actuals" match "standards"? — NO → **Initiate system to show performance against standard**

↓ YES

Have you scope for more advanced work with people? — NO → **Can you find post to satisfy you and employee?**

↓ YES

Are people capable of tasks set with better skills, knowledge habits and attitudes you can develop? — NO → **Can you find post to satisfy you and employee?**

↓ YES

Establish training spec. — NO → **Place them**

↓ YES

Implement programme

Can you find post to satisfy you and employee? → YES → **Place them**

→ NO → **Dispose, in everyone's interest**

BLAKE

Ted on
Management by Objectives

Ted was well ahead of his time in introducing management techniques. Management by Objectives did not really become evident in this country until the 1970's yet, at the first Recreation Management Conference in Feb 1969 there was Ted Blake, not only the sponsor of the Conference but also giving a talk on Management by Objectives.

The Content of his talk which follows is as relevant today as it was more than thirty years ago when it was delivered.

WHAT IS MANAGEMENT BY OBJECTIVES?

Management by Objectives (MBO for short) is a continuing systematic style or way of executive life dedicated to improving performance by insisting that all job holders:

- Name names
- Define, quantify, integrate and agree targets with the names in terms and language understood by all
- Give and obtain a commitment to achieving targets in accordance with a firm time table
- Agree dates at which results are to be appraised, and if found short of target, answer the question 'What are you going to do about it?'

Recreation Management
10th – 13th February 1969
National Conference and Exhibition
Crystal Palace, London SE19
Sponsored by Nissen

Management by Objectives
An introduction by Ted Blake

- Draw up job and job improvement plans with superiors based on the difference between agreed performance and actual results
- Review at specified times progress achieved with improvement plans then adjust training and up date targets accordingly.

It is result rather than task orientated concentrating on just Key Result Areas (KRA's) leaving the remainder of managerial activity, probably about 80%, to the discretion of the job holder. Although the KRA's probably only take up about 20% of the manager's total activity they probably account for 80% of the results achieved.

Because everything is spelt out, pinned down with the total personal involvement, commitment and agreement of all concerned, MBO can be tough, very tough. Nobody is much interested in the 'displacement' of peripheral activity that, along with occupational hobbies, have little or no bearing on the Key Results the job holder is expected to achieve. Because job holders have to set down their own objectives and commit themselves to a time for achievement MBO has been described as a Do It Yourself Hangman's Kit.

WHAT IS IT NOT?

It is not new. Socrates probably started it with his dialectic questioning method aimed at improving self knowledge. It is not deductive – the leader does not explain and then verify or 'prove' – it is inductive – all people involved question and then discover. It is not a tool for day-to-day control nor a substitute for specialist functions and techniques. It is not easy or quick to implement as it usually involves radical changes in attitude and outlook. It is not a style that can survive and grow for long without total commitment from the top.

WHAT ARE OBJECTIVES?

They are realistic written records setting out in quantified and measurable terms agreed targets for achievement within specified periods of time. They indicate direction for action and the form the action should take. They take account of all likely internal and external constraints to eliminate excuses for poor performance. They fit in with both the long term, high level objectives of the organisation and its lower level, short term objectives. They record who has agreed to do what, how the results will be measured, the deadline for achievement and the date for review.

CAN ALL OBJECTIVES BE QUANTIFIED?

No, but more can than perhaps we think. For example improving the quality of instruction given to recreation classes at the Centre could increase the number of people wanting to take part; reduce the number of accidents; increase reservoir of new instructors or helpers; reduce equipment maintenance costs; increase number of skills mastered, awards gained or matches won; increase donations, public support and official appropriation of more money, equipment, land staff, etc.

HOW DOES MBO MEET THE MANAGERS NEEDS?

Very well, not just as well as it meets his staff's needs because it answers two questions everybody wants answered. What do you want me to do? What performance is expected of me? By applying the three stage rule of happiness which we can state as:

1   Giving people the opportunity to choose and participate in really challenging activity, defined in terms they agree and believe, and appropriate to their ability.

2 Giving people the support, guidance and interest necessary to achieve success.

3 Giving recognition and rewards for achievements made, measured against a performance and time scale they agree is realistic.

BUT DON'T MOST MANAGERS HAVE OBJECTIVES?

Right, in a vague way they do. But how many can say now, immediately:

a) Precisely what these objectives are without wanting to change their minds 30 minutes later?

b) What time scale they are operating on?

c) That the objectives have been discussed and agreed with all people expected to cooperate in their achievement?

d) That all constraints have been considered so fully to make the objectives so realistic that there are no personal excuses left for non achievement?

e) That the objectives not only specify the ends but they also analyse and determine the means?

f) How they will review and reward performance or agree improvement plans?

Well not many perhaps, because it is not that easy. Right again, but if determining of objectives is the key to management and you will have the will to succeed you also have the will to manage. Everybody wants to know, few want to learn. Nobody claims management is easy but this creates the opportunity for those with the will to master it.

WILL MBO SOLVE ALL OUR PROBLEMS?

No. But it will help people to better visualise and define what the problems are and so improve their chances of overcoming them. It will help avoid the problems that should never arise. It will help close the objectives gap between all staff from top to bottom – rarely does a subordinates assessment of desirable objectives in a job immediately and entirely coincide with those of his boss before MBO is practised. MBO will provoke and renew job interest, and until you have this it is ridiculous to talk about improving communications. MBO is communication in every good sense of the word. Everybody likes to be told what is happening but they like better to be asked to help make it happen. MBO aims at self fulfillment by 'job enrichment' through increased personal involvement, responsibility and recognition. Increased wages, fringe benefits, good working conditions alone do not make people happy, they just stop them being unhappy. It has been said that Doctors know a lot about illness but very little about health. Similarly most managers are well able to prevent or cure misery at work but how many actively seek to contribute to happiness? Both health and happiness need working on pretty hard. The extent to which people will devote themselves to the objectives of any outfit will depend, like exercise, on the fun or satisfaction they get out of it. Personal objectives and business objectives must be in harmony – out of the same hymn book – for the best results.

HOW DO WE START MBO?

With ourselves. MBO, like most exercise, can be a difficult and sometimes painful affair. Experience is the best school but the fees are high. Our superiors and subordinates are probably too busy keeping up with the demands of their own jobs as they see them to have the time or non-subjective view needed for defining precise objectives and quantifying measures of performance.

We would be doing less than our job as managers if we were prepared to commit our helpers to an untried experiment we are reluctant to attempt ourselves. Very large businesses overcome the difficulties of getting MBO started by appointing a special staff adviser skilled in the Socratic technique of asking the right questions that can lead staff to 'discover' what the objectives can be and how to attain them. The Recreation Manager will have to be his own Socrates. He can succeed very well if he questions himself. Value and standards are caught more than taught and example is difficult to ignore.

WHAT ARE THE FIRST PRACTICAL STEPS?

1   Identify, isolate and write down the Key Results Areas (KRA's) of your job. These are your main responsibilities. Check with your employers or superiors; it is possible they may have different ideas about what your main responsibilities should be.

2   Break down each of the KRA's into no more than four INDICATORS or measurable sub divisions of your main responsibilities. They are the tasks or actions you take to discharge your responsibility in each Key Result Area. Check these again with superiors and colleagues.

3   Set against each indicator the RESULTS you are achieving at this time. Record these results in quantities, percentages, ratios, times or dates. This will give you the base line you need from which to measure your achievements for the future and it's a worthwhile exercise.

4   Set against each current result you have recorded your OBJECTIVE, goal or target for improvement, e.g. up 2%, down to 1 to 40, ready in two months, confirm in 48 hours, etc. As a beginner take short term objectives first as a check on how realistic your approach is and how reliable it might be when you start on longer term objectives. Mark these objectives in pencil first. Let's see why.

5   Set against these objectives the constraints that could prevent you from achieving your objective, along with the superior or colleague support and information you must have to overcome the constraints. After checking whether or not you can count on the support and information you

must have, you may have to rub out and alter your objective. Alternatively restrict the experiment by choosing objectives entirely under your control and free of outside constraints.

6   If your objective does not have a time – give it one. Reducing overheads by 12% may be okay if it is understood that this means a year but 1% a month might be better. Confirm or decline all bookings promptly is good, but saying within 48 hours. is better. Have a target, date or time.

7   The time for achieving your base line results and the target date for achieving your objective is called the improvement period. At the end of this improvement period you, or you and the boss or subordinate, if it has been a corporate exercise, review performance. The discussion must be very frank between boss and subordinate with the aim of finding out what is wrong rather than who is right. If performance is less than expected the question, 'What are you going to do about it?' has to be asked, answered and agreed.

8   The question, 'What are you going to do about it?' must be followed with other helpful questions aimed at getting the listener to see for themselves what the possibilities for improvement are. From this discussion a short term improvement plan and training programme, if needed, are outlined and later implemented. Will this be desirable in all cases? Not if the job holder's ability, energy or motivation (their standards – not what incentive

they have) are below the level expected for the job, training will not help. The door or a change of job may be the only answers. Better to know this early rather than late.

SUMMARY

The Management Committee, or authority employing the manager of the leisure centre will discuss with the manager how to make the best use of the assets they have in land, buildings, money, equipment and people and agree on one or more non-overlapping overall guiding objectives. The objectives will be written, realistic, quantified, measurable, time tabled, constraint considered, action indicative and agreed.

The constraints will have been checked against the support and information required to overcome them and firm commitments made that if the objectives are agreed, the support and information required are also agreed and certain to be forthcoming.

The overall guiding objectives will be explained to all the leisure centre staff in terms they can clearly understand, believe and want to take action on. Ideally they will know what business they are in and what business they are not in.

Discussion will begin in the leisure centre with the manager and his assistants working out what the key results areas or responsibilities are for the achievement of the overall guiding objectives. The Key Results Areas will be broken down into indicators, or the actions that will be taken to discharge the responsibilities.

Constraints will be considered and mutual support and information agreed to overcome them. Short term objectives are finally agreed and everybody goes to work – no excuses for not achieving or not helping – no ifs and buts after the agreement. Je m'excuse, je m'accuse.

Hourly or weekly paid employees are informed of what the supervisors hope to achieve – not by being told but by being asked, 'Is this possible?' 'What do we need to do?' 'What can you do?' 'What standards do you set yourself?' 'Could we write them down?' 'What time or date could we set for their achievement?' 'What management support do you need?' etc. etc. The answers may be all complaints – fine – examine every complaint, ask – 'What would you do?' 'Would that work?' 'If we put that right can you

achieve?' 'Do you agree we can now do it?'

We all know where we are going, how we are going to get there, how our speed is being measured, how our progress will be recognised and who we can count on in trouble.

WHERE CAN YOU GET HELP WITH MBO?

You can help yourself by reading the many books on the subject, attend seminars and courses run by the many professional Institutes and the British Institute of Management, show the free sponsored films, start discussions with other managers or authorities, call in management consultants, call your own conference or seminar, think more of asking than telling what can be done. Don't rush things, MBO takes time.

To get anybody Excited about any hobby, job, sport, game, activity:-

<u>4 KEY INGREDIENTS</u>

1   A Meaningful Goal
2   A way to keep score so people can SEE and Measure their progress
3   Control over achieving the goal
4   Meaningful rewards – size
      Timing – Unexpected – Public – Peers
      Impact – Frequent – Recent, Probability and In-consistency

---

If it can't be **Measured**...

... it can't be **Managed!**

FEEDBACK !

<u>Peter Drucker</u> says...

"When you have 186 objectives... nothing gets done.

I always ask... What's the ONE thing you want to do?"

Change your view

We can see things in two ways, said Ted.
Just turn this upside down and see the result!

Performance Measurement

Ted believed in colour and fun

The Interval

The first half of the book, Act 1, has introduced some of Ted Blake's repertoire of Management Skills. 'Ted on Time Management' demonstrated that the efficient use of a manager's time is of crucial importance in getting things done effectively, without the strain and stress – a concept he called Lazy Management!

'Ted on Leadership' illustrated that the best managers need to understand themselves, their colleagues, customers and their employers and to lead the organisation towards its goals. 'Ted on Communication' introduced the slogan A.I.D.A. to gain attention, hold interest, stimulate desire and instigate action. 'Ted on Delegation' clarified that delegation is not simply off-loading tasks, but creating for the manager the time for dealing with key priorities and, in parallel, enhancing the professional growth and confidence of staff.

'Ted on Training', underlined the importance he placed on professional training and development, the need to instil in staff the essential management skills and to motivate and inspire them to provide excellent services.

The first half closed with a paper presented by Ted entitled, 'Management by Objectives' which illustrated the maxim; 'If it can't be measured, it can't be managed'.

At this point in the book, readers will be well-versed in the lateral thinking and simple solutions Ted brought to seemingly complex situations and management problems. The second half of the book, Act 2, presents Ted's ideas, more or less verbatim, in the form of a series of humourous illustrations, as in the first part, but with editorial comment only, leaving the reader to enjoy the humour, pick up the message and make the connection to good management. This half of the book consists of three main scenes: I Marketing; II Selling and Winning Customers; and III Quality and Customer Service. This is followed by a miscellaneous selection of vintage Ted Blake illustrations, jokes and quotations.

Ted on
Marketing

Ted Blake's name is synonymous with marketing. He was a walking, talking example of marketing in action. A man filled with a promotional mix! Ted moulded the customer-oriented management style of the early pioneers of Recreation Management in the late 60's and early 70's.

Ted believed that everything you do in running a service-oriented organisation is part of your marketing philosophy. For that reason marketing, in one form or other, popped up in nearly every presentation he made.

Visitors to the Nissen sports equipment factory in Essex, whoever and whatever they were, would be welcomed in the foyer by a hand-written and personalised message, letting the visitor and all the staff know they were expected and welcome. Ted would say "create an atmosphere in which you stand the best chance of satisfying the customer".

Ted placed great importance on recognising the value of both market and asset based marketing. This, his philosophy went, means that you constantly plan to respond to ever changing customer needs. However, at any point in time you have also to make the most of your existing assets in the marketplace – your sports hall, fitness gym or gymnastic equipment product since these can only be changed or improved incrementally over a period of time.

Ted presented marketing to his audiences in different ways at different times, to suit the mood or emphasis of the time. However, he very rarely covered one of the many management topics presented in a lifetime of 'training and entertaining" his clients and audiences without placing emphasis on putting the customer in the forefront of marketing activity.

The marketing illustrations that follow are a selection from Ted's wonderful library. They reflect how Ted conveyed good marketing practice in simple statements but at other times helped managers grapple with complex situations with his famous diagrams. They also show how he used humour to convey fundamental marketing messages.

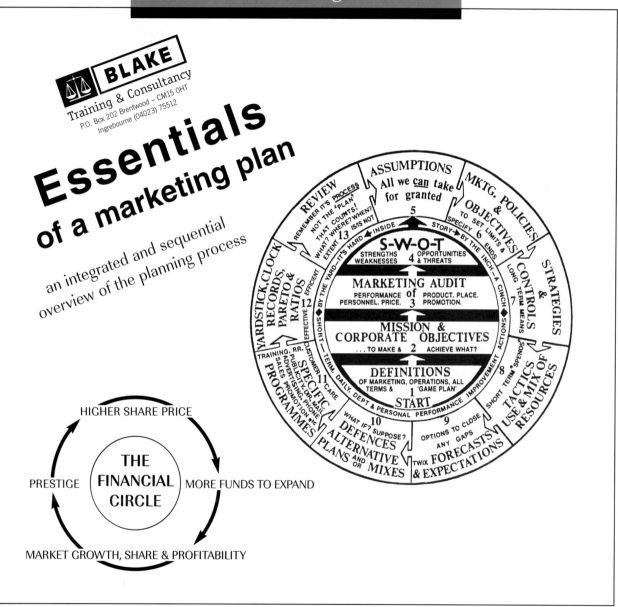

BLAKE
Training & Consultancy
P.O. Box 202 Brentwood – CM15 0HT
Ingrebourne (04023) 75512

Essentials
of a marketing plan

an integrated and sequential
overview of the planning process

THE FINANCIAL CIRCLE

HIGHER SHARE PRICE

MORE FUNDS TO EXPAND

MARKET GROWTH, SHARE & PROFITABILITY

PRESTIGE

MARKETING P-S-T

- **Policy**...sets **Limits**, Value for money, Priorities in Asset use

- **Strategy**...includes Controls as it sets Goals & <u>allocates</u> Resources; 7 concerns are What-How much/many-By Whom-By When-Where-Why & at Which cost?

| Economy |
| Effecti-veness |
| Efficiency |

- **Tactics**...sets **Methods** & uses Resources...P.R., 5 Media--advertsg-Mail-Promtn-Personal

⚖ BLAKE

Marketing Means...
working Smarter—not Harder!

How "Smart" are Your Objectives?

S — Specific

M — Measurable

A — Agreed

R — Realistic

T — Time Bounded

A DIFFERENT WAY TO LOOK AT LEISURE MARKETING?

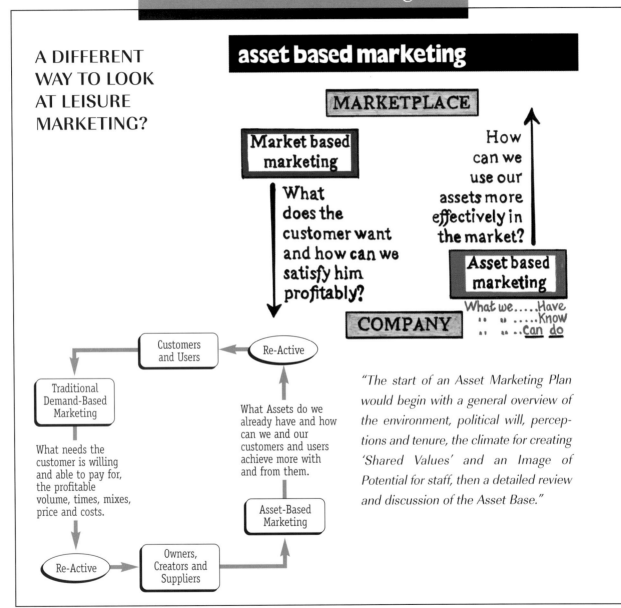

asset based marketing

MARKETPLACE

Market based marketing

What does the customer want and how can we satisfy him profitably?

How can we use our assets more effectively in the market?

Asset based marketing

What we.....Have
"   " .....Know
"   " ...can do

COMPANY

Customers and Users

Re-Active

Traditional Demand-Based Marketing

What needs the customer is willing and able to pay for, the profitable volume, times, mixes, price and costs.

What Assets do we already have and how can we and our customers and users achieve more with and from them.

Asset-Based Marketing

Re-Active

Owners, Creators and Suppliers

"The start of an Asset Marketing Plan would begin with a general overview of the environment, political will, perceptions and tenure, the climate for creating 'Shared Values' and an Image of Potential for staff, then a detailed review and discussion of the Asset Base."

BLAKE

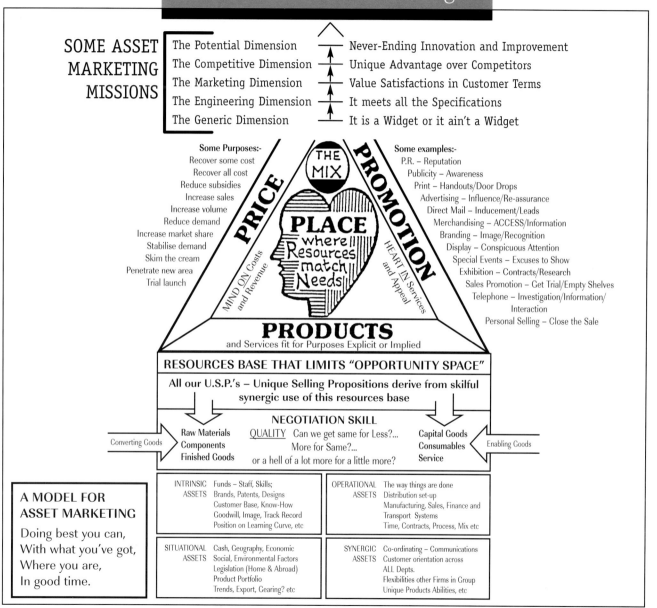

SOME ASSET MARKETING MISSIONS

The Potential Dimension — Never-Ending Innovation and Improvement
The Competitive Dimension — Unique Advantage over Competitors
The Marketing Dimension — Value Satisfactions in Customer Terms
The Engineering Dimension — It meets all the Specifications
The Generic Dimension — It is a Widget or it ain't a Widget

Some Purposes:-
Recover some cost
Recover all cost
Reduce subsidies
Increase sales
Increase volume
Reduce demand
Increase market share
Stabilise demand
Skim the cream
Penetrate new area
Trial launch

THE MIX

PRICE — MIND ON Costs and Revenue

PLACE where Resources match Needs

PROMOTION — HEART IN Services and Appeal

Some examples:-
P.R. – Reputation
Publicity – Awareness
Print – Handouts/Door Drops
Advertising – Influence/Re-assurance
Direct Mail – Inducement/Leads
Merchandising – ACCESS/Information
Branding – Image/Recognition
Display – Conspicuous Attention
Special Events – Excuses to Show
Exhibition – Contracts/Research
Sales Promotion – Get Trial/Empty Shelves
Telephone – Investigation/Information/Interaction
Personal Selling – Close the Sale

PRODUCTS
and Services fit for Purposes Explicit or Implied

RESOURCES BASE THAT LIMITS "OPPORTUNITY SPACE"

All our U.S.P.'s – Unique Selling Propositions derive from skilful synergic use of this resources base

NEGOTIATION SKILL
QUALITY   Can we get same for Less?...
More for Same?...
or a hell of a lot more for a little more?

Converting Goods →
Raw Materials
Components
Finished Goods

Capital Goods
Consumables
Service
← Enabling Goods

INTRINSIC ASSETS	OPERATIONAL ASSETS
Funds – Staff, Skills; Brands, Patents, Designs Customer Base, Know-How Goodwill, Image, Track Record Position on Learning Curve, etc	The way things are done Distribution set-up Manufacturing, Sales, Finance and Transport Systems Time, Contracts, Process, Mix etc
SITUATIONAL ASSETS	SYNERGIC ASSETS
Cash, Geography, Economic Social, Environmental Factors Legislation (Home & Abroad) Product Portfolio Trends, Export, Gearing? etc	Co-ordinating – Communications Customer orientation across ALL Depts. Flexibilities other Firms in Group Unique Products Abilities, etc

A MODEL FOR ASSET MARKETING

Doing best you can,
With what you've got,
Where you are,
In good time.

"Marketing is all about full employment – especially for those with jobs. Only those with full employment can create jobs for those without. Marketing looks outward from the organisation to where its opportunities and revenue are found rather than just inwards where the costs and the routine lie."

MARKETING AND SELLING – WHAT'S THE DIFFERENCE?

For a start, marketing is buying and selling.

A frequently heard assertion is "Marketing is just Selling with knobs on", and a frequently heard question is, "Well, what is/are the difference(s) between Selling and Marketing?" Set out on the following page are some thoughts for you to compare, contrast and prioritise. If you can't, as the marketing person, differentiate between Marketing and Selling, then you don't have the delusions of grandeur we're often accused of, you have delusions of adequacy! ... Far worse.

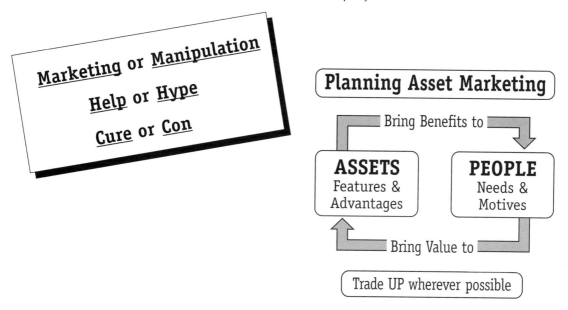

Marketing or <u>Manipulation</u>

<u>Help</u> or <u>Hype</u>

<u>Cure</u> or <u>Con</u>

Planning Asset Marketing

Bring Benefits to

ASSETS
Features &
Advantages

PEOPLE
Needs &
Motives

Bring Value to

Trade UP wherever possible

Marketing and Selling

ATTRIBUTE	MARKETING creates DRILLS for Engineers	SELLING offers HOLES to Prospects
Parameters	Wider/broader/later/creating and keeping customers	Narrower/deeper/now/finding and closing prospects
Composition	Includes: product development; pricing; distribution; and other forms of promotion additional to selling	Is limited to personal or telephone contact or direct off-the-page purchasing
Policy Level	Strategic i.e. it allocates resources to meet marketing's only 4 objectives	Tactical – It consumes time and other resources to meet selling's 3 main objectives… contact time, productive time, lucrative time
Means and Tools	Segmental, co-ordination of products, price, place and promotion (Macro Approach)	Individual AIDA – Getting personal attention, holding their interest, arousing desire, getting action (Micro Approach)
Focus	Customer delight/astonishment	Existing products and services
Perspective	Get company TO MAKE what customers require and beyond	Get customers TO TAKE what company has already
Listens to	What customers want to achieve	What customers want to buy or do
"E" Factor	Effectiveness i.e. Doing the right job	Efficiency i.e. Doing the job right
Reciprocity	Provides selling with products, segments, leads and back-up	Provides marketing with contacts, revenue, feedback and reality
Time Scale	Present and long term	Present and short term
Market Change	Development (Frog), many options, high flexibility	Growth (Bigger Tadpole), few options, low flexibility
Stretch	Optimise cash flow, return on investment, inventory and accounts receivable levels	Maximise inventory range level and turnover (i.e. speed of asset turnover)
Force Direction	Pull – Getting USERS to ask for	Push – Getting distributors to stock
Product Life Cycle	Pre-natal to demise or resurrection	Childhood to maturity
Immediate Ends	Never-ending all-round improvement	Orders in, or bums on seats
Attitude	We should lead taste and innovation	We should follow current demand
Yardstick/Slogan	Creating more goods and services that won't come back to more people who do	Nothing happens until somebody sells something, so ASK for the order
Media	Publicity, P.R., advertising, sales promotion, packaging, merchandising, display	Personal, telephones or direct mail, investigating, identifying and interacting
Financial Outlook	To MAKE money	To TAKE money

Everybody lives by buying something

Everybody lives by selling something

The Institute of Marketing defines Mktng as...

..the Management process responsible for Identifying, Anticipating & Satisfying Customer Requirements "Profitably"

WHAT IS MARKETING NOT

⊙ It is not a bunch of Techniques & Gimmicks

⊙ You don't learn Mktg.....you FEEL & Imagine it.

Getting Ideas about the
3 parts of the Marketing Mix

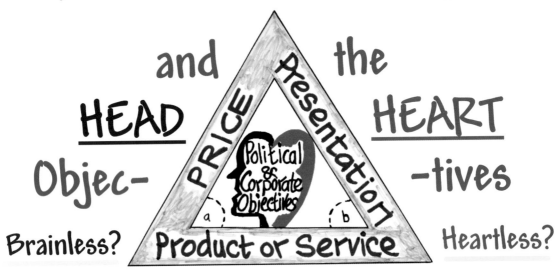

and   the

HEAD   **HEART**

Objec-   -tives

Brainless?   Heartless?

PRICE · Presentation · Product or Service

Political & Corporate Objectives

... and Whats the △ and Position in Market?

 BLAKE

Place

Distribution Segment Niche Fragment?

Physical Distribution

Marketing Channels

Customer Service

Facilities
Inventory
Transport
Communication
Unitisation
= Total Costs

Supplier
agents?
distributors?
retailers?
Customers
Users

I want...
value • best?
loose • packed
now • just in Time
Attention
Importance
understanding

P.R. & ADVERTISING

| **ALL** entities **Have** | **SOME** entities <u>choose</u> to **advertise**. |

P.R. ....the aggregate of attitudes towards...and perceptions of... the entity, held by people who have...or may <u>later</u> have...some <u>impact on its fortunes</u> whether <u>they choose message or not!</u>

FIRMS SHOULD BE MARKET .....NOT MARKETING LED

NO AMOUNT OF 'MARKETING' CAN RESTORE TO PROFIT A PRODUCT OR SERVICE THAT PEOPLE ARE NO LONGER WILLING &/OR ABLE TO BUY i.e. NO DEMAND 3M 5 Year, 50% Plan

Communication in NOT a separate part of the job – it is the job. Operating by objectives and management by inclusion are communicating. If done properly everybody does know other peoples aims and abilities as they've worked on them together to make sure there are no surprises.

BLAKE

69

MBWA The Bunker Mentality

MBWA (Management by Walking About)

... Mind your own business.
THIS is how I like it!

Can it Ever work?

**Designers Design
- Managers Inherit**

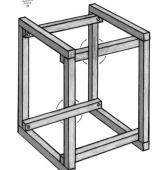

Sport Increases the Intensity of Life

Quality is like Golf!

Aim:- Complete a Process without "Waste" & disappointment
Challenge:- To master common & specific Variabilities
Requires:- Full Set of Clubs 14?
Stages:- Unconscious Incompetence → Conscious Incompetence → Conscious Competence → UnConscious Competence
Success & Improvement depends on Never-Ending Commitment.

Near enough is not good enough

Techniques are all too Mechanistic. If you rely only on Techniques you are not a Manager but a technician.

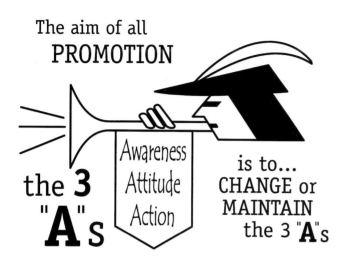

The aim of all
PROMOTION

the **3** **"A"s**

Awareness
Attitude
Action

is to...
CHANGE or
MAINTAIN
the 3 "**A**"s

EVERYBODY BUYS DRILLS BECAUSE THEY NEED AND WANT DRILLS – half right again, Blake!

People don't buy Insurance, they buy Peace of Mind; they don't buy Xmas trees, they buy Festivity; Retailers don't buy Manufactured Goods they buy Profits.

So, don't sell what the product, or service IS... translate its features into Benefits and sell what it DOES.

People don't want Drills... they want **HOLES.**

PR

by Socrates
(470-399BC)

The best way to gain a "good" reputation is to try to Be...all you wish....to appear.

P.R.

Deliberate, Planned and Sustained Effort to Create and Maintain Mutual Understanding between an Organisation and its Publics ... a better definition ?

– Spreading the TRUTHS about your Outfit so that people...
KNOW, BELIEVE AND LIKE you more

HOW in Advertising. Headline "How to..."

- tell how Fresh things are. Greengrocery
- make your car last longer-sell easier. Garages
- get <u>urgent</u> items delivered Yesterday BRS
- have Colour in your Garden 52 weeks of year Nursery
- find hidden treasure in your home ? Antique
- make the <u>most</u> of what <u>seems least</u> } Dealer
- host the PERFECT dinner party   A small private
- become a Cordon-Bleu cook for a day Caterer
- find the ideal FIREPLACE for Your home Design-Make
- re-kindle the HEART of your living room Installers
- win friends & influence people Improvement Courses
- to Close more Sales? Find more customers Books &
- make sure you're not living with a thief Db. Glazing

USE HOW-WHY-WHO WHEN-WHERE

WHY is more flexible than "How to...."

- Why SIGNAL has mouthwash in the stripes
- Why Bomb inventors now want to ban it
- Why 100,000 came to Joe's....?......
- Why Porsche can't catch a Mazda
- 10 Reasons why Betty Bakes are Best
- Why I took my case to Sue Grabbit&Run
- We do 67 checks—Why so many?
- Maradonna tells why he always wears
- Why Jesus saves&the Pope invests

FREE (almost) Advertising
Some Prime Sights...

- Company Stationery - Tag Lines (Slogans) Invoices - Comp. Slips - Franking - Labels
- Company Vehicles - doors - sides - stickers
- Coy. Buildings - Main Rd? Railway? Posters?
- Calling Cards - Where's __SALES__ message?
- Meeting Rooms - Reception areas
- Moving Messages - Windows - Cars
- Answer Machines & Awareness Info.

76

Advertising: A Checklist.

1 Is it CLEAR <u>who</u> you're talking to?

2 Is it CLEAR <u>what</u> your offer is?

3 Is it interesting...in matter & manner?

4 Is it <u>INSTANT</u>? Picture? Headline? Posters? = Nutshells.

5 Is the "<u>Promise</u>" believable? Who says so?

6 Right length? T.V. ½ Min = 60 words = 2/sec. Press-more time. Letter-most.

7 Is it CLEAR what reader has to do? What?

8 HOW are you <u>PROVING</u> your case? Evidence. Try & see?

9 How many OTS's are likely? Why? When

10 How will you prepare to 'measure' it?

In MARKETING I've often confused what people NEED with what they WANT

Every parent knows their kids need "sensible" shoes, but what adolescent daughter wants to be seen wearing them?

If they don't want what you think they need you cannot even GIVE it to them – let alone SELL it to them!

Nobody can see anything as it is... ONLY AS THEY ARE. You may think your service scores 9 out of 10. The customers may think otherwise. How do you know? Check it!

Throwing an eleven foot rope to a man drowning twenty foot away is not more than meeting him halfway!

Advertising a SERVICE... say "We...our..."

- Already have **50** 'Blue Chip' Customers
- ..staff are the best in the field
- case histories **PROVE** our service un-beatable
- have **X** years experience in **Y**(or All?) fields
- call on you with many samples of our work
- are Different in a **+** way. Sales of the Un-expected
- wide range of skills gives you many choices
- can **SHOW** how to make **YOUR** money go further
- deliver Same for Less - More for Same - LOTS more..
- like Prospective Clients to call & "look us over"
- very handy to reach - 24 hour call any day
- are utterly reliable - **YOUR** peace of Mind
- staff 😊 a lot - are Cheerful & Adaptable
- **HERE** is our Phone - Telex - Address (Branches)
  contact Ted, Bill, Jean or Sue .

NOW tell Prospect what you want them to DO

*"Business improvement through marketing
By the yard it's hard....... By the inch it's a cinch"*

*"If the customer ain't gonna get any **REAL BENEFITS**
(e.g. selling refrigerators to Eskimos)
then you are not a true salesman – you're a CON MAN!"*

*"Communication is measured by what happens. Small goals
start motivation, small consequences maintain it ... and that
is no small thing...break down hopes, fears, targets into a
small number of REALISTIC targets".*

*"Marketing means seeing **everything** through the
customer's eyes. He is not always right ... but only he has the
right to be wrong".*

*"Marketing communication's practical aim is to help people
make better decisions, and make it easy for them to say
yes!"*

TED'S MARKETING FINALE

Above all, Ted demonstrated by his highly amusing and
thoughtful presentations that *"word of mouth gives you the
largest, most enthusiastic and credible sales force".*

Ted on
Selling and Winning Customers

ACT II Scene ii

According to Ted, everybody lives by selling something, ranging from Popes, Princes and Prime Ministers to Plumbers, Porters or Prostitutes. These are some of his thoughts and writing on salesmanship.

Ted worked in a business environment. In business Selling is the most important job but so little thought, time, care, training and organisation is devoted to it.

How frequently throughout any organisation does the following question get asked.

> Is what I am doing or about to do, getting us closer to our objective or making us money?

"I DON'T WANT TO SEE ANY CRAZY SALESMAN – CAN'T YOU SEE I'VE GOT A BATTLE TO FIGHT"

BLAKE

To be successful in selling, like marketing, you need objectives that are **SMART**

- **S**pecific
- **M**easurable
- **A**ttainable
- **R**ealistic
- **T**ime Bounded

Nothing changes – anywhere – until someone sells something. All improvements have to be sold.

The Skills of Selling are important for all. We need to know.

- What have we for sale?
- Who are our customers?
- Why should they buy from us?
- When will their needs change?
- Where else can they do better?
- How are we selling?

Your most important product is yourself. Customers buy people first and everything else is secondary.

The selling job to be done.

Sell:

- Yourself
- Your staff (management by consent)
- Your colleagues (win allies)
- Your owners (capital providers)
- Your suppliers (you both need the best)
- The users (direct consumers)
- The buyers (the indirect consumers)

SELLING .... getting Customers to want what the Company has.

MARKETING .... getting Company to produce what the Customer wants

Asset flexibility is the difference

WANTS .... The founder of Revlon said... "In the factory we make Cosmetics... while in the store we sell HOPE".

Effort is required in selling. It's being:

- Nicer than is natural
- More patient than is natural
- Listening more than is natural
- Asking more questions than is natural.

Make it nicer for people to do business with you. Remain in control of your **attitudes**. No matter what our **feelings** are, our **attitude** will always be showing.

Feelings are facts in selling. Customers can't see our feelings. Customers use appearances, images and attitudes to form judgements about realities.

You will lose customers by not being polite, by being abrupt or rude. It is important to remember also that receptionists, secretaries are also your customers. Always be polite. It is still the most acceptable hypocrisy.

Making the Sales Call

Plan your call. Write it all down first, rehearse how you will reply to questions. Stay in control by answering questions with further questions.

Don't make the mistake of trying to sell your product before you have sold the interview i.e. yourself.

If your customer says he is not interested, it means only one thing – you haven't said anything interesting. Don't give up until you are talking to the right person. In fact never give up, never think that it is impossible.

Selling means helping people to make better decisions. So make them feel good, happy and secure about the decisions you have helped them to make.

> # Persuasion
> The man who moves ahead is the man who has <u>Any</u> talent to get <u>Others</u> to see things <u>His</u> way, believing it was <u>Their</u> way-Anyway

People don't buy it for what it **Is**	They buy it for what it **DOES**
Insurance	Peace of Mind?
Xmas Trees	Festivity?
Shoes	Dry feet, Pretty Feet, Comfortable Feet, Warm Feet etc Envy?
Sport	Fun & Adventure with Security Romance?
Exercise *(which – if any "problems" does it* **CURE?**	Security, Power, Esteem, Variety, Social Acceptance to become what they THINK THEY ARE? Buy off your Guilt?

Selling is hard work. It is important to:

- Make it easy to say YES and
- More difficult to say NO.

This is the overriding sales technique.

Once you have gained an order, don't think your job is done. What happens after you have gained an order is as important as what happens to get an order.

Selling is a two fold job

First to deliver all we have led the customer to expect and secondly by our manner to create a further demand for it.

Quality of Service

Be around to check on things at or around delivery time. If things go wrong don't shift the blame just put the problem right.

Sales people may tell three lies

- It's all my fault
- It's been a pleasure to meet you sir.
- You're absolutely right.

Stay close to your customers. Don't let them surprise you by switching to a competitor. Keep surprising them by giving unexpected attentions. Not just a Christmas Card. Keep in touch with them throughout the year. 'Have a happy Guy Fawkes Day.' Send them congratulatory card 'Just heard the good news about the order you got from Brazil.' If all other things are equal, this might be your unique selling point.

Pricing is important. If a customer tells you it's too expensive, he means he doesn't want it enough. Demand is what people are able and willing to pay for.

Value for Money

$$\text{Value} = \frac{\text{Function}}{\text{Costs}}$$

$$\text{Perceived Value in Leisure and Recreation} = \frac{\text{More \& Better Satisfying Experiences} \quad \text{ie QUALITY}}{\text{TOTAL cost in Time Money, other Losses in Opportunity, Dignity, Respect etc}}$$

ACT II Scene ii

You should undertake a Value analysis

How can you get:
- The same benefit for far less cost
- More benefits for the same cost
- Many more benefits for a little extra cost.

Factors that can affect our market position

To add value we can make our products:
- Bigger
- Simpler
- More compact
- More reliable
- More convenient
- More desirable
- Easier to maintain

Can our delivery be:
- Quicker
- More frequent

Can our service be:
- Friendlier
- More targeted

Can our literature be:
- Better written
- More visual

Never give away unnecessary pricing concessions. Never give anything away without getting something in return. Be proud of your product. Always keep your customers informed.

Remember when a chicken lays an egg it clucks all round the yard. When a duck lays an egg it slinks away in silence. Ask yourself, 'Who buys ducks' eggs?'

Do not enter into Dutch auctions with your competitors. You may cut your competitors throat but it will be you who will bleed to death.

The salesman who gives 5% discounts on a product on which there is a 20% mark up will find that as a result he has no money to service the needs of customers. You will discover that to give 5% discount you will need to find 30% more customers to get back to where you were. You won't be giving away discounts. You will be giving away customers.

The moral is never give away unnecessary concessions because you lose the respect of those customers when you have to take those concessions back again.

How to lose Customers

The best way to lose customers is not to find them in the first place. Don't sit in the office. Get out there and find more potential prospects.

Creating customers is one skill, keeping customers is another.

Like finding a partner: 'Kissing is what gets them, Cooking is what keeps them.' (Classic non-PC Ted)

30 RANDOM JOTTINGS FROM TED ON SALES – HOW AND WHY PEOPLE BUY

1 People buy for their reasons not ours. So find these reasons.

2 Sales are made by questions, not statements.

3 People buy first on emotion and then justify on logic. Get feelings right.

4 There's no such thing as value, only perceived value.

5 People do not buy Features or Advantages, but Benefits. Sell F-A-B.

6 People buy when they have M-A-N. Money Authority and Need. Check your prospect is a MAN. Ask is there anyone else who should be in on this meeting.

7 Qualify your prospect as a M-A-N or part of a D-M-U i.e. Decision Making Unit. Double glazing salesmen always talk to husband and wife together.

8 If price is an objection it means they don't want it enough. So sell enough.

9 If you are 10% out on price that's good because it means 90% of the job has been done. All you have to do is sell the 10%.

10 Your prospect may be part of a larger D-M-U or S-P-A-D-E so you have five people each with a different reason to buy i.e. S for Starter, P for Professional Purchaser, perhaps only interested in price, A for Adviser, éminence grise in the background perhaps – a consultant – or some other adviser; D for Decider – the person who signs the cheque or has override e.g. the M.D.; and E is for End User – find them all and sell to them as they all have distinctive influences.

11 Support any statements the customer makes i.e. your courses are expensive. Don't argue, just say 'Yes, they are expensive.'

12 Withhold support from any customer statements that don't take us close to our objective which may not be a sale – it might be some other commitment like a demonstration etc.

13 Anything they write down they will believe and understand, of course.

14 Bear in mind the four No's... they have no trust in you, no need, they are getting no help, and they're in a hurry. Act accordingly.

15 Customers don't care about what you know until they know you care about them.

16 If they say ' I want to think about it.' Agree with them and ask 'If people say that in my experience it means they are unsure about some things. Would you agree with that Mr. X'? If he says 'Yes' as I am sure he will, just say, 'Could we run over those things you are uncertain about' and list them. Then say, 'Is there anything

else we have not thought of? If he says 'No' say, 'Can we line them off now?' and draw a line. If he keeps inventing new things, you're on to a loser so don't waste time – leave. If there's a genuine addition ask again and underline it. Then say 'Mr X, if I can satisfy you on these five points, can we go ahead?'

17 Sometimes they don't buy because the Salesperson doesn't actually Ask for the Order.

18 'Tis said that customers will not say 'Yes' until for some reason or another they have said 'No' four times. Circumstances change. Persistence pays. 44% of sales people give up after the first No. 24% after the second No, 18% after the third No. That leaves 14% or even less who really get the business.

19 People do not buy from people they don't like if all other things are equal. People do buy from people they do like, who seem clean, fair, caring, interested, etc.

20 If the Boss tells you the price is non-negotiable, say, 'OK can I have a list of what is negotiable?'

21 People buy from Sales Persons with an ABUNDANCE MENTALITY i.e. who think on a WIN/WIN basis, who work hard to find options that satisfy both sides.

22 In biology there is a law – the Law of Requisite Variety that states... Organisms with the greatest variety of response options are most likely to control situations in which they find themselves. So project all situations, have an abundance of options.

23 People buy from Sales people who welcome objections as an opportunity to sell again the benefits. Buying signals are any sign of interest Up or Down. They wouldn't object if they were not interested in the product or topic.

24 People buy from sellers who appear Professional. They don't sit down till invited. They don't chatter about other customers or vendors. They are always on time. They DWYSYWD (Do What You Said You Would Do). They take, rather than post quotations so they can answer questions. Correction, they take proposals, not quotations.

25 A Quotation normally has specifications, price and delivery on the front, and on the back all the conditions of sale in small print – 27 reasons why they shouldn't buy. A Proposal starts off with a summary of what the Customer has said they want to achieve (not what they want to do). Then proof is given that this can be achieved by the seller with reasons. If the legal adviser insists on a quotation and conditions of sale, then do that but attach the proposal to it.

26 Feelings are facts. People like to feel that they have bought rather than been sold.

27 Selling is creating and delivering goods that

won't come back to customers who will. Think not of current value of the customer's order but the long term value of the customer who will keep coming back if the quality and the ethics have been pleasing.

28 The definition of Quality is the customer's definition. Sales people must ask appropriate questions to ascertain this definition very early on and note it for inclusion in the proposal.

29 We never get a second chance to make a first impression. If the phone keeps ringing unanswered and when answered is treated in a pompous supercilious manner, the sales may never even get under way. Phrases like, 'Can I help you?', 'What is it about?', 'Does the M.D. know you?' 'He/she can't talk to everybody', 'We're very busy you know', are common responses from the Sales Prevention Department. Everybody must be ready to talk to customers. If not now, then by firm appointment.

30

Ted on
Quality Customer Service

Although as we enter the twenty-first century the term 'Customer Care' may be a phrase which everyone can recognise, interpret and embrace, in 1970 that was not the case. The terms 'Customer' and 'Care' were not necessarily synonymous particularly in the newly emerging sport and leisure management industry. In the early days we referred to 'users' and unfortunately often treated them with the same disdain which we might apply to the word 'user' today.

Ted Blake changed our thinking or perhaps more accurately confirmed to those who had a commitment to providing excellent customer focused services that they were on the 'right track!' Long before we had heard or seen the flamboyant performance by the American Management 'Guru,' Tom Peters, we had listened in anticipation to and been consumed by laughter by the Managing Director of Nissen International, a diminutive 'fire ball' with a cockney accent, called Ted.

He brought the meaning and relevance of the term 'Customer Care' to us all, irrespective of our level within the organisation. Through his inimitable style of presentation with its emphasis on 'bite sized' chunks and 'humorous' strap lines, he 'convinced' those who were unsure of and reassured those who were committed to the 'creed' of customer care.

This chapter focuses on Ted Blake, the mentor as it relates to his message on Quality Customer Service.

The following extracts from Ted's presentation to the John Fenton Organisation's 1996 National Sales Convention serve to illustrate his thoughts and although some of the language might seem inappropriate in these days of 'political correctness', the compelling combination of sound theory and humorous delivery provides a potent and forever relevant message.

Thank you, John, Good morning everyone.

John has warned me that YOU are probably the most intelligent audience I will ever have the privilege of talking to.

This is very good for me as it means I can go much faster than is possible with ordinary people.

In fact I'm going to time myself to see if that's true.

I'm using my old Dad's watch. He gave it to me on his deathbed. He charged me ninety quid for it ... so I gave him a cheque.

Now people of your intelligence and experience

QUALITY
Service....is <u>Not</u> giving Customers all they are entitled to..

...it <u>Is</u> giving them <u>more</u> than they are entitled to.

I know that's true. I had the same problem. I lost many customers for health reasons. They got sick of me ...

> **IT COSTS FIVE TIMES AS MUCH TO FIND NEW CUSTOMERS AS TO KEEP OLD ONES**

Doesn't the surly, indifferent attitude of some Council employees make you wish you could switch suppliers?

I visited the Fitness Room at our local sports centre. I got no attention, no help or encouragement from the weight-training instructor ... He looked at his wit's end, but that way he couldn't have travelled far. I looked in his eyes from time to time ... but there was nobody driving.

He was poncing around all the time, admiring himself in all the mirrors ..

He was as strong as an ox – almost as clever. I left and I took two others with me .....

It's a fact ... many Local Authority sports centres lose one third of all their customers every 12 months by taking 'em for granted.

And think of all the customers that shop assistants lose with their couldn't care less attitude. I went into a shop recently to buy some perfume for my wife. Again, I got no attention, no help or advice. They just don't have any pride in their work.

don't need to attend a seminar like this to be told you can lose existing and present customers by ...

• Poor Quality...
 there's only ONE definition of Quality
 The customer's definition
• Late/Short/Damaged/No Delivery... or
• If you deliberately, or even unintentionally, screw 'em on price ... or
• You've obsolete products and services.

O.K. So it's obviously easy to lose customers with poor quality, unreliable delivery and overpricing, but a survey by McGRAW HILL, the largest book publisher in the world, revealed that...

> **63% of customers switched suppliers because they FELT they were being taken for granted, i.e THERE WAS A SUPPLIER ATTITUDE PROBLEM.**

BLAKE

> **GALLUP SURVEYED 970 SHOPPERS AND FOUND 'FRIENDLY STAFF' RATED OVER TWICE AS HIGH AS LOWER PRICES AND SO-CALLED QUALITY GOODS.**

And what about those STREAKERS? They run across the rugby pitches ... they run across the cricket pitches, and now they're running across the tennis courts. If they had any pride at all .. THEY'D WALK ... and think of the extra customers that could bring in.

Awful Service	Good/Adequate Service	GREAT Service
Negative Word of Mouth	NO Word of Mouth	Positive Word of Mouth

What We Get Paid For

WHAT
1 Delivering the Services Promised and so Expected...i.e. THE MATTER! and

HOW
2 By our MANNER OF DELIVERY create greater Satisfaction, Publicity & Demand for it.

We never get a second chance to make a first impression. **Customers are won or more easily lost in the first 30 seconds maximum.**

First impressions give customers confidence. Could you have any confidence in a doctor whose potted plants are dying?

It's easy to Lose Customers by not trying ENOUGH. Joe Girard, top American Car Salesman claims ...

44%	of ALL Salesman give up after the	1st	NO
22%	" " " " " " "	2nd	NO
14%	" " " " " " "	3rd	NO
12%	" " " " " " "	4th	NO

So, after 4 No's .. Not interested/No money/No need/Want to think about it, etc.

– 92% of all car salesmen are out there dead on the forecourt.

– Only 8% are still alive and pitching.

Yet surveys have shown time and time again, 60% of all customers don't say 'Yes' until they've said 'NO' (in some form or other) ... 4 times.

What does all that mean? It means the 8% of salesmen still living and pitching, could get 60% of the orders.

opened his briefcase and put on his running shoe samples. No. 2. Said, "What are you doing that for? You can never outrun that lion." No. 1. Said, "I don't have to ... All I have to do is outrun you."

Don't try to beat the customer. He is only looking for a fair deal... Outsmart ... OUTRUN THE COMPETITION.

Remember, with any initiative you want to take it's ALWAYS easier to get forgiveness after the event than permission before. HAVE A GO ... Don't suffer from BOTTLE FATIGUE.

It's easy to lose customers by treating them as ADVERSARIES to beat down.

Two competing salesmen were in a remote area of Kenya to sell sportsgear. The buyer had been delayed so they decided to take a stroll outside the compound. Suddenly a lion rushed out of the jungle. No. 1. salesman

93

It's easy to lose customers if you don't know how to make a cold call ... "Good morning, Mr. Smith. Have I told you yet about our new Reciprocating Fondulators with Cadnium Hardened Grovel Pins?"

"No, you haven't Ted and I'm so grateful to you for that. Goodbye."

To fail to prepare ... is to prepare to fail

And never, no matter how much they try to prevent you talking to their Boss, be rude to secretaries. They can be very influential and are often the real power behind the DRONE. I got so frustrated once I shouted, "Is there an Idiot on the line?" and a polite and gentle voice confirmed ... "Not this end, sir."

It's easy to lose customers if you don't sharpen up your negotiation skills. "How much are those cream buns?"... "Two for 50p" ... "How much is one of them?" "30p." "O.K. .. I'll take the other one."

All professional Buyers insist on Price Breakdowns. Avoid where possible, be ready if necessary. Bundle your Price and Benefits whenever you can.

Never let a prospect surprise you with half an order. I wasn't very pleased with one of the sales managers I had. I thought he was losing orders, so I waited until he went out of the room and took to answering his phone. When he came back, I said "While you were away from your desk (implying he had no right to go to the toilet on Company time) I sold 76 table tennis tables to Liverpool." "Oh," he said, "Great!" How many nets did you sell 'em? "They didn't ask for any nets." "Well, how many bats did they want?" "They didn't ask for any bats." "Well, what about balls? How many gross did they ask for?" "They didn't ask for any balls." "Well how are they going to play table tennis on all those tables you sold them without nets, bats and balls?" I had not only lost half the order, but I'd lost respect of this manager .. and the buyer ... who never came back.

ASK FOR THE ORDER ... the full, complete order. There is no better ... or maybe other ... time than when given half an order. Know ... and sell their FULL NEEDS.

Customers can't surprise you with half orders if you have thought out contingency plans to back up your first plans if they don't work. Let me explain what I mean by a Contingency Plan ... The big game-hunter told his Safari tourist, "Today we are going out to capture gorillas .. alive ... to send back to zoos in Europe. Would you like to come along?" "Yes." "O.K. ... then you carry this shotgun and I'll explain what happens. Gorillas are usually found among the low boughs of the trees. I then put this ladder up into the tree. I climb up to get as near to the gorillas as I can ... there is nothing to fear as they are very gentle creatures and vegetarian. I then take out my air pistol and fire an anaesthetic dart at the gorilla. He falls out of the tree and as soon as my bulldog hears the thud, he rushes forward and grabs the gorilla by its private parts. He holds him there until we can tie the gorilla up and put him in the cage." "That seems simple enough," said the tourist, "but if we're going to capture them alive, what do I need the shotgun for?" "That's my contingency plan," said the big game hunter. "That's for you to shoot the bulldog should I fall out of the tree first."

There's no excuse for telling stupid jokes like that unless there is a useful sales message to remember, and that is ... You'll never fail if you have two plans for broken appointments, changes in specs, calls for special discounts, customer objections, unanswered quotes/proposals, etc.

Example of Contingency Plan in action ..
– "How much is that oil painting?"
– "£300." ... and if they don't flinch at that, say ..
– "Plus £50 for the frame" and if they don't flinch at that, say
– "£20 for packing, postage and insurance".
  Einstein (one of the two greatest thinkers of this century. Modesty prevents me from revealing the name of the other) said,

"Nothing stands alone. Everything is relative to something else." For example: Everybody's current sales level is directly related to their total Company's average Customer Contact Time, not just the sales people's Contact Time, but everybody's Contact Time. You can't sell anything without Customer Contact. So. If we're achieving our current level of sales with an average of all staff Customer Contact Time of, say 10% total time, if we could raise that average by just 2%, we would increase our sales figure by 20%.

Keep them INFORMED POLICY
Give Reasons for Delay, etc
" Regular Up-Dates — Old
SHOW concern — ♥ = Worried Families
Answer Questions – clearly, concisely Disabled, etc
Be AVAILABLE to Establish Facts
Be AWARE "they" can be Angry Worried
Don't Over-React Emotional Labour Be Proffessional
Don't Promise what can't be met.
Phone-Acknowledge-Eyes-Names-Note

... and Ted used to add, "And learn to spell"
Spot the mistake?

The easiest way to lose customers is to lose contact with them. They don't care you know ....until they know you care. So ... SHOW 'EM. You have no time to lose ... only a great deal of money. What have you done for them LATELY?

In Sales ... being Professional is Important but being Trusted is ESSENTIAL. In the Kingdom of Camelot, Sir Lancelot got all King Arthur's orders to pass on, and this gave him great job security, commissions and prestige.

When King Arthur left to fight in the Crusades, he locked Queen Guinevere in her chastity belt and gave Sir Lancelot the key, saying "Take care of this Lance ... you know what I mean don't you?" "I know what you mean, Guvnor," said Lance.

But King Arthur had only got about 15 leagues down the M5 when Lancelot came galloping up in the fast lane and waved the King onto the hard shoulder. "What's the problem?" asked the King. "Well, you have given me the wrong key, Guv," said Sir Lancelot.

TACT ... It's often dangerous to show you know too much, but rarely that you CARE enough to respect confidences. Those who chatter to you, chatter of you. It's so easy to lose Customers if you will keep "giving them away".

Poor understanding of other people's position can lose us many customers. Nobody can ever see anything as it is – only as we are ... position-wise...

The Greek Navy were on manoeuvres in the Aegean Sea on a dark foggy night ... when the lookout man on the command vessel called out, "A strong light approaching on the starboard bow." The Admiral asked, "Is it coming straight ahead or moving astern?" "It's coming straight ahead." "Right, flash them a signal, "Change course by 20 degrees." Back came the signal from the light ... "You change course by 20 degrees." The Admiral was incandescent at this and ordered. "Flash another signal – I am an Admiral ... Change course by 20 degrees." Back came the signal "I'm an ordinary sailor ... You change course by 20 degrees." The Admiral exploded. "Signal – I am a Battleship ... Change course by 20 degrees." Back came the signal, "I am a Lighthouse ... change course by 20 degrees."

The moral of this story is ... Before you venture out into the dark and misty prospecting area, do some pre-approach research. Check your, and their, positions, and above all, don't make any assumptions or you may lose more than customers. If you don't know where you're going how will you know when you're lost?

I used to behave like the Admiral. When I was young I was known as the Business Typhoon – all wind and swirling around in circles. I was doing for Salesmanship what King Herod did for Mothercare.

My wife once asked me, "Ted, has anybody ever told you you're wonderful?" "Well," I replied, "Now you ask ... no they haven't." "Well," she asked, "Then where on earth did you get the idea from?"

Always listen to those who've bought "your line" so often before.

Never let your M.D. serve on your exhibition stand. You'll get Admiral-type output like ... "Can I ask you a couple of questions?" "Of course you can, sir. What's the second question?" "Can I have a quick

THE CUSTOMER'S ALWAYS RIGHT, BENSON. MISINFORMED PERHAPS, INEXACT, FICKLE, BULL-HEADED, IGNORANT, EVEN ABOMINABLY STUPID, BUT NEVER, NEVER WRONG!

The Customer is NOT always Right...

..but only he has any right to be wrong!

word please?" "Yes, how about Velocity? Will that do?"

He will also OVERSELL ... "This machine will cut your production time by 50%." "Oh good. I'll take 2 of them and cut it out altogether." "A good idea sir. Just O.K. this order."

My first M.D. was like that. He lost us thousands of customers. Very devout, he always knelt in his own presence. He had a modestly fitted office ... just a few full-length mirrors and a throne. He's dead now ... he was knocked down and killed by a motorboat while he was out walking.

Sadly, although they say practice makes perfect, we don't always improve with age ...

First we forget Customers' names ...

Then we forget their faces ...

Then we forget to pull up our zip ...

Then we forget to pull it down ...

Do take care – An embarrassed customer is a lost customer

MBWA means Management by Wandering Around ... Wandering around catching people out ... doing something RIGHT and then giving immediate appreciation and thanks.

However, sometimes people get the wrong slant and think the idea is to catch staff out doing something WRONG. Dutifully, one M.D. wandered around, saw a young lad sitting on a packing case in the warehouse smoking a fag. "How much do you earn a week?" he asked the kid. "About 120 quid." The M.D. pulled six 20's out of his wallet, shoved them into the kid's hand and said "Take this, get out, and never show your face here again." The M.D. then went to the Warehouse Manager and told him he had fired one of his employees. "He wasn't one of our employees," the Warehouse Manager said, "He was just a kid delivering a parcel and waiting for a signature."

Just a quick thought here. Never tell Lies – unless it's one of your real strengths. Always tell the truth - then you've got less to remember. Honesty is not the best Policy, it's the only Policy. Here's an example:- "Ted, your competitors are up to 20% cheaper than you." "They certainly are, Sir, and we cannot quarrel with that. After all, they know the value of their stuff far better than we do."

Here is a common sales situation ... "Are you the man who dived off the end of the Pier and saved my son when that giant wave washed him overboard?" "Yes I am, Madam," "Well where's his cap then?"

Don't ever let Idiot demands like that upset you. They come with everybody's territory.

Talking of idiots ... never hire one as they multiply. Once you have hired one you immediately have two on the staff ... You and him.

There is no quicker way to lose customers than to mishandle Complaints. Write down now and follow this magical 5 Point Plan I'm going to give you for handling complaints which are, by the way, the best, cheapest and fastest market research you can ever get. Right, here we go ...

Step 1 Acknowledge their right to complain by saying something like "I can see you're upset madam, therefore it must be important" ... or if he is shouting, "You were talking so fast then sir, I couldn't get a note of it and that is important for us".

Step 2 Sorry. Say "I'm sorry IT happened." Give no excuses, no justification, mention no personalities.

Step 3 Glad. Say quickly after Sorry, "I'm so glad you brought it to our notice so we can make sure it never happens again."

Step 4 Positive Options. Say "I personally would like to do something positive about this. Here's what we could do ... Option a, b, c, d, e, etc.

Step 5 Happy. This is the magical question. "What do I have to do right now to make you happy again?"

Never back off or be indifferent to customer Complaints ... they are real gold if you handle them well. Never fall back on the Conditions of Sale or bring in lawyers. Nobody loves lawyers. How can you tell the difference between a dead lawyer and dead

cat on the motorway? There's skid marks in front of the cat.

Once in Tunisia, in a village outside Algiers, I came across three of the local lawyers buried up to their necks in sand. I asked the local Head Man "What's the problem?" And he said, "We've run out of sand."

"I'm near my end now – in more ways than one. I'm so old now I can remember when the Dead Sea was merely unwell. I've mentioned never do this and never do that, but now I'm going to say Never ever, when considering creating sales possibilities – NEVER SAY NEVER. Everything is possible."

Taken from John Fenton's
1996 National Sales Convention

Providing **Quality Customer Services** has become the key feature of service delivery during the last decade. As a consequence one of the great challenges to any organisation is to ensure that all members of the team share the same under-pinning values in terms of providing high-quality, customer-orientated services and products.

YOUR ATTITUDE IS SHOWING

It is often difficult to provide a consistent standard of Customer Care throughout the various levels of an organisation. Ted's presentations appealed to a wide audience because of his use of humour and 'punchy,' easy to remember phrases and as a consequence the message was usually universal and relevant to all, particularly in the context of work in the leisure industry.

"Your Attitude is Showing" – An often referred to statement and a powerful message in the context of delivering Quality Customer Services.

This message was used to remind everyone of their responsibility to present a positive welcoming image at all times and in whatever method of com-

continued on page 102

HOW TO DEAL WITH DIFFICULT PEOPLE

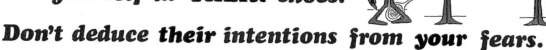

Put yourself in THEIR shoes.

Don't deduce their intentions from your fears.

Don't blame them for your problem. (How *You* Feel)

Discuss each other's perceptions. — Exactly

Look for opportunities to act inconsistently with their perceptions.

Give them a stake in the Outcome by making sure they participate in the process.

Face-saving: Make YOUR proposals consistent with THEIR values.

munication. This message was reproduced in 'sticker' form and displayed in strategic locations throughout the organisation to remind staff with an irate customer that the customer is always right and they should present a 'positive attitude' whatever the provocation.

SERVICE QUALITY

Service quality was arguably the most important feature of Ted Blake's personal and professional philosophy. Ted often quoted the response of an American astronaut on returning from the moon landing when asked:-

"Which single thing out of all things gives you the <u>most</u> confidence?" He replied "Knowing that none of the contracts for my equipment were awarded to the lowest bidder."

This philosophy was the cornerstone of the Nissen Sports Equipment Company – Ted would readily accept that they were not the cheapest but would always contest that they provided the best quality and few people argued with that claim.

Ted used the following 5 dimensions of Service Quality diagram and allocated a service weighting and customer rating to the 5 dimensions which are reliability, responsiveness, assurance, empathy and tangibles. The underpinning message was 'RIGHT FOR THE JOB – RIGHT FIRST TIME.'

Ted applied the 5 dimension of Service Quality to individual roles as Host, Consultant and Seller. The message is clear. We all have the opportunity to fulfil all of these roles at some stage in the Selling Sequence but the emphasis may change depending upon the circumstances and the response required at the time. We should however all be aware of the components which make up the Selling Sequence of a Quality Service.

continued on page 107

Service Quality

means doing the right thing right the first time... everytime... <u>ONCE!</u>

RIGHT FOR THE JOB

the only
QUALITY
circle

RIGHT FIRST TIME

Beware... if people have no right to fail... you'll nevet get anything new!
"A mistake is merely evidence that someone tried to do something!"

5 DIMENSIONS OF SERVICE QUALITY

SERVICE DIMENSION (Weighting of service dimension in overall customer rating, derived from regression coefficient)	DEFINITION	Remember ... customers cannot judge our intentions ... only our behaviour **FOCUS GROUP COMMENTS** **i.e. Feedback from specific and important Customer Groups**
reliability (30 percent)	The ability to perform the promised service dependably and accurately	"Sometimes they take care of your problems too fast. They fix your truck and two days later you have to take it back for the same problem. Sometimes I think they could be a little more attentive and fix the problem permanently." *Truck leasing customer*
responsiveness (25 percent)	The willingness to help customers and provide prompt service	"When I want to put a new policy into effect I get a quick response. But when I have a problem ... forget it." *Business auto customer*
assurance (20 percent)	The knowledge and courtesy of employees and their ability to convey trust and confidence	"I need the feeling of security. When I receive information from a competing company I would like to talk it over with my agent for reassurance that I still have a good policy." *Auto insurance customer*
empathy (15 percent)	The caring, individualized attention provided to the customer	"I would like to be able to communicate with the insurance provider who understands that while their actuarial tables are in black and white, life is played in shades of grey. I don't want to talk to an insurance person who is reading out of a book." *Auto insurance customer*
tangibles (7 percent)	The appearance of physical facilities, equipment, personnel, and communication materials	"Do something to the service areas of dealerships. They are cold, stark, uninviting places." *Auto repair customer*

QUALITY SERVICE - THE SELLING SEQUENCE

 **host**

1 YOUR ROLE AS A HOST

- Ensure Environment is RIGHT
- Acknowledge Customer with Eye Contact
- Give a Greeting and a Smile
- Ask <u>HOW</u> may I help you?
- Talk about Customer 1st. Programmes 2nd.
- Be Positive - "Can Do" - in approach
- Judge yourself on your ability to create and maintain
  - good relationships with others
- LEARN and USE CUSTOMERS' <u>NAMES</u>
- Never see an Environment defect without doing SOMETHING about it
- Act "AS IF"... the Centre was your own home

SALES ARE DIRECTLY PROPORTIONATE TO CUSTOMER CONTACT TIME

The reason people pass one door
To patronise another store,
Is not because the busier place
Has better silks or gloves or lace
Or better prices, but it lies
In pleasant Words and Smiling Eyes.   *Anon.*

 BLAKE

QUALITY SERVICE - THE SELLING SEQUENCE

consultant

2 YOUR ROLE AS A CONSULTANT

- Over Phone always ask where they heard of you, etc.
- Know not only the Features of all the Facilities but the BENEFITS for each type of Customer
- Use <u>OPEN</u> Questions to determine
  NEEDS - WANTS - INTERESTS - TIMES
- Be ever-ready to give - or get promptly - <u>answers</u> to their queries
- <u>Listen</u>, Observe, think always of...
  HELPING THEM TO MAKE BETTER DECISIONS
- Remember YOU - AND <u>YOUR</u> EXPERTISE are the Facility in the Customer's mind
- Rehearse how to offer ALTERNATIVES
- Get all the Product Training you can
- Earn and maintain the TRUST others show in you by asking your advice and suggestions

SALES ARE DIRECTLY PROPORTIONATE TO CUSTOMER "PRODUCTIVITY" TIME i.e. all the <u>information</u> you need to make a sale.

105

<u>Q</u>UALITY SERVICE - THE SELLING SEQUENCE

Don't try to sell
Features, sell
the <u>BENEFITS</u>!
to <u>THIS</u> customer

seller

3 <u>YOUR ROLE AS A SELLER</u>

- Select and show suitable Activities <u>AND</u> appropriate ALTERNATIVES
- Anticipate and pre-empt OBJECTIONS
- Clear up DOUBTS and Welcome Objections
- Use any Objections as a 2nd Opportunity to SELL AGAIN by countering with Benefits
- Watch out for "<u>BUYING SIGNALS</u>" i.e. <u>ANY</u> Interest – Positive or Negative – then <u>OFFER</u> a demonstration, a trial, a membership, etc.
- Always show RELATED activities as additional options
- If an Activity is fully booked offer an ALTERNATIVE – <u>with</u> an incentive to try
- <u>CLOSE</u> the Sale by asking a Closing <u>Question</u> – Closed questions requiring a DECISION. If you don't try to close the sale you've only done part of the selling job.

SALES SUCCESS IS DIRECTLY PROPORTIONATE TO LUCRATIVE TIME – <u>CLOSING</u> ORDERS.

Ted's dimensions of Service Quality were always 'linked' to the creation of "profit". He was essentially a business man who recognised that providing high quality equipment and after sales service produced customer loyalty resulting in profit and growth. The inter-relationship between service quality and profit is illustrated by the Quality Customer service and The 6-link Service Profit Chain.

(see following page)

TED'S TOP TIPS FOR QUALITY CUSTOMER SERVICE

"There's only one definition of Quality
– The customer's definition."

"Our role should be to sell goods and services which don't come back to customers who do."

"The Quality of the product or service is remembered long after the price has been forgotten."

"Quality can be defined as "Fitness for Purpose."
Joseph M Juran.

"People buy on Emotion and then justify with logic."

'Sports centres, pools, theatres and gymnasia are merely warehouses holding tangible and intangible products that have no value except that brought to them by customers'

QUALITY CUSTOMER SERVICE
AND THE
6-link service-profit chain

HOW we **GET**

1. *Profit and growth* **driven by** *customer loyalty*
   It costs 5 times as much to find a New Customer than to keep an old one who will buy More of More.

2. *Customer loyalty* **driven by** *'external' service value*
   There's no such thing as Value... only **PERCEIVED VALUE**. In Surveys **friendly staff has rated higher** than facilities, price or range.

3. *External services value* **driven by** *employee productivity*
   i.e. the **ADDED VALUE** each employee gives to the premises, equipment, their Time spent in **MEETING OBJECTIVES** or **MAKING/SAVING MONEY**.

4. *Employee productivity* **driven by** *employee loyalty*
   NEVER TAKE EMPLOYEE LOYALTY FOR GRANTED... It has to be earned with Security/Significance/Consultation, etc

5. *Employee loyalty* **driven by** *employee satisfaction*
   The **A → B ← C** of motivation
   PRIDE & SELF ESTEEM through Personal Goal Fulfilments with Positive Consequences. Any Behaviour not reinforced will extinguish itself... **REINFORCE SELF RESPECT**

6. *Employee satisfaction* **driven by** *'internal' service quality*
   e.g. In workplace and procedure design "tools" to **ENABLE AND AUTHORITY TO ACT AND** the Efforts Example, Sensitivity, Flexibility and Judgement of Bosses.

WHY we **NEED**

Quality means not only **DOING THE RIGHT THINGS** but also **DOING THINGS RIGHT**... and that usually means doing things in the right order or **SEQUENCE**... so for every single **ACT**
BEGIN WITH THE END IN MIND!

 BLAKE

"You are charged with desertion in the face of the enemy"

Training Books Before the event and there'll be less need for Rule Books After the event.

Rules = Doing things Right   Training = Doing Right things.

The Art of Ted

The art of Ted and the use of illustrations

'A picture tells a thousand words'

In addition to his outstanding skills and competence as a motivator and communicator, Ted was a talented artist who prepared highly complex and colourful illustrations to support his verbal message. He also used apposite work of others.

The illustrations were always direct and poignant and reinforced the underlying message with the strong use of humour, irony and topicality to make the point. The visual images achieved impact and always retained the interest of the audience.

The illustrations presented a kaleidoscope of colour and humour which ensured that the subject was indelibly printed in the brain for easy recall of a message which was universally understood and appropriate to the environment.

Ted learned long before us that the average person recalls 30% more when humour is used:

"The play was a great success, but the audience was a failure."

"They never drink coffee before his after dinner speeches as it may keep them awake."

The "Half Life" concept...

...the length of time that will elapse before Half "your" knowledge & skills are...

.. Obsolete

The above illustration is the only self-portrait of Ted in the whole of the immense collection of overhead transparencies

"Whenever opportunity knocks, instead of getting on his feet to open the door, he complains about the noise."

BLAKE

► WORDS

The Lord's Prayer contains 56 words, the Ten Commandments 297, the American Declaration of Independence 300. The European Economic Community Directive on the Export of Duck Eggs contains 26,911 words.

WHY do Staff Resent, Resist & Defeat Outside Imposed System Changes?

- Lack of Trust in Motive & Outcomes.
- Implied Criticism of Present Efforts.
- If any Success the New System will get the Credit.
- If any failure staff will be blamed for not co-operating with System.
- Can't see anything in it for me
- Can't see anything of me in it.

The History of Progress is founded on Dissent

Don't Smother it-Use it

Remember... what is NOW well proven..
..was ONCE only Imagined
...and most ideas start with just a
..Minority Vote of 1

A CENTIPEDE with gout visited a wise old owl for advice on his condition. Said the owl: 'You must change into a mouse so that you only have gout in four legs, not 100.' 'How do I do that?' pleaded the centipede. 'That's your problem,' said the owl, 'I just make policy.'

Sport <u>improves</u>...
...the Quality of Life?

Sport <u>increases</u>...
...the Intensity of Life!

Anger, determination, exhilaration, anticipation, disappointment, bitterness, suspense, frustration, etc

"Mavis, meet the boss."

Is Idealism enough?
Is the Rec. Manager
'up the Pole'...
...because he
cannot yet put a

£ Value

on the
Social Benefits
in the Choices
he is offering
the Cost Conscious

Galileo AD1633. Died 1642   Pope

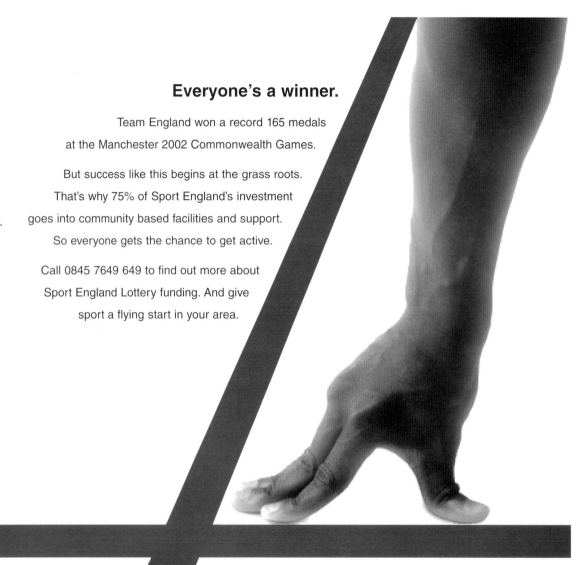

Everyone's a winner.

Team England won a record 165 medals
at the Manchester 2002 Commonwealth Games.

But success like this begins at the grass roots.
That's why 75% of Sport England's investment
goes into community based facilities and support.
So everyone gets the chance to get active.

Call 0845 7649 649 to find out more about
Sport England Lottery funding. And give
sport a flying start in your area.

SPORT ENGLAND
The nation's biggest supporter

www.sportengland.org

 BLAKE

C The Chief Culture and Leisure Officers Association is delighted to be associated with this publication. Ted Blake was well known to our members as the leading "Guru" in the leisure industry for his views and concepts on a variety of areas such as customer care. Ted's thoughts back in the 70's reflect today's initiatives such as Best Value.

CLOA
CHIEF CULTURAL & LEISURE OFFICERS ASSOCIATION

Leicester City Council are proud to sponsor the 'Contribution to Sport' Award. Our Sports Services strive to raise the profile of sport throughout the community.

Leicester City Council

CCL believes that the publication is a wonderful tribute to Ted who brought his own unique humour to leisure management and motivated everyone who was fortunate to hear him present.

*Roger Bottomley OBE
Chairman, CCL*

CCL

For the experience

Of working alongside the Ultimate, Man Manager, for receiving the education and relentless uncompromising help with family and business matters, we remember with immense fondness, thank and give tribute to "The Guvnor", and of course the joke about just wearing baggier suits.

Jacqui and John Griffiths
Nissen 1970/83

*Solution of puzzle
on page 24*

BLAKE

TED'S USE OF MUSIC AND POETRY

Ted used music and poetry to attract attention, create interest and emphasise the point he was making. Favourite poems used were *'IF'* by Rudyard Kipling, *'Paracelsus'* by Robert Browning and Charles Kingsley's bleak poem:

> *When all the world is old, lad,*
> *And all the trees are brown;*
> *And all the sport is stale, lad,*
> *And all the wheels run down;*
> *Creep home, and take your place there,*
> *The spent and maimed among:*
> *God grant you find some face there,*
> *You loved when all was young.*

Many of the classic standards of popular music were used to illustrate a theme and reinforce a message, particularly when presenting a personal perspective.

The classic standards by Frank Sinatra, Andy Williams, Harry Secombe and their rendering of *'To Dream the Impossible Dream'*, *'Razzle Dazzle Em'*, *'Make the World a Little Younger'*, *'High Hopes'* and *'If I Ruled the World'* were particular favourites, although Frank Sinatra's *'My Way'* almost became Ted's signature tune.

Andy William's version of *'To Dream the Impossible Dream'* held particular significance, as it was the music which was played as part of his presentation to the first Recman Conference in 1969 when it was retitled *'The Leisure Manager's Quest'*.

And so, we reach the final curtain!

"Ted has made a host of friends ... a never-ending list of people influenced by him who are proud to have known him.

The word used most often to describe Ted is Dynamic. He was one of Life's characters, indifferent to the material things, with an amazing Abundance Mentality and Generosity of Spirit. He went through Life with courage, shunning fashions and fads, airs and graces. Calling a spade a spade, and with his commonsense down-to-earth messages, he helped people to make better decisions ... a generous legacy benefitting so many."

Jean Mackenzie
PA to Ted for 41 years

Curtain call

"And now the end is near and so I face the final curtain
My friend I'll say it clear
I'll state my case, of which I'm certain.
I've lived a life that's full,
I've travelled each and every highway
And more, much more than this.
I did it my way."

[Words by Paul Anka;
Music by Claude Francois and Jacque Revaux]

Ted was a great admirer of Frank Sinatra's 'My Way' and we hope that, on the preceding pages, we have shown that he did indeed have a very clear and uniquely personal way of looking at things and tried to use it to benefit others.

It's tempting to speculate on what Ted would have made of current developments in the industry; it's fairly certain, for instance, that the word 'culture' - encompassing not only the arts, but sport and recreation also - would have had him reaching for his revolver! He is likely to have been encouraged by the growth and increasing professionalism of leisure management training and education, although he may have been frustrated by some of its non-practical content and by the continuing lack of uniformity. He would undoubtedly have been disappointed at the low status that many facility managers currently 'enjoy' in local government, but would have revelled in the business opportunities presented by the burgeoning health and fitness industry. It is probably not even worth speculating what he would have made of current national policy towards sport and the continuing travails of government agencies and the development of national facilities.

But it is not for those of us left behind to speculate on the mind of a business genius, enjoyable though such speculation might be!

We've tried, through the medium of this book, to remind those who knew Ted what an inspiration he was and to introduce some of his ideas to a new generation who may never have met him or had the privilege of hearing him speak. Above all, our intention was to pay tribute to a great MANager, one whose name rightly belongs at the forefront whenever the origins of the leisure profession are discussed.

We set out, not to try to imitate him, for to do so would be impossible, or to interpret him, for there is no 'Ted Blake Unified Theory of Leisure Management'; rather, we've tried to collect and present his ideas, as closely as possible to the original concept, without the benefit of his unique 'voice'. We hope that by doing so, we have helped to preserve his reputation and to place it where it belongs - high up in the Pantheon of Leisure Management thinkers and teachers.

In Act One, we looked at Ted's approach to people: people as customers, people as subordinates and the self-image of people as developing managers. We explored how Ted contrasted the rounded, self-aware and target-orientated 'MANager' and his opposite, the incompetent, unaware and undirected 'manGLER'. The varying impact of the service provided by them, their facilities and their staff on the ever-important customer, was a unifying theme which linked the process of leisure management to its delivery.

In Act Two, we looked at the importance in a people-orientated business of marketing, selling and setting personal and organisational objectives. We saw how some of the successful techniques employed in manufacturing and other industries can be applied to a service business such as leisure. We looked at this through the eyes of someone who made and sold the equipment which was the hardware of our industry, but who understood the software of managing resources to satisfy the end user.

So, where do we end?

Ted took his curtain call after a long, full life. We can still hear the applause to his wonderful presentations, perhaps with a favourite song of Ted's playing:

'The Impossible Dream' from 'Man of La Mancha':

> *"And I know, if I'll only be true*
> *To this glorious quest*
> *That my heart will lie peaceful and calm*
> *When I'm laid to my rest*
> *And this world will be better for this*
> *That one man, scorned and covered with scars*
> *Still strove with his last ounce of courage*
> *To reach the unreachable stars"*

When asked by his long-serving Secretary/PA, Jean Mackenzie, "What would you like as your epitaph?", he quoted what was printed at the bottom of his notepaper, ***"He helped people make better decisions."***

We hope that this book will help its readers to do likewise.

May 2003

Ted Blake: a tribute

"Don't tell 'em that you know, show 'em that you care"

Although the word is often misused, in Ted's case he really was a legend in his own lifetime and a legend during the short history of modern leisure management. Those of us who can go back that far will remember his inspirational presentations at the Recreation Management conferences and other events from the mid-seventies and into the early eighties, all drawn from his extensive experience with Nissen (trampolines among other things not cars!). His anecdotes and amusing aphorisms, reinforced by his unique illustrative talents have stayed with us ever since.

"Don't tell 'em that you know, show em that you care"; "Ten years' experience can be one year's experience repeated ten times"… and obviously many more.

Ted was one of the first evangelists of the need for the customer-focused approach in the fledgling recreation management profession and raised our awareness to the importance of systematic performance management.

This collection of abstracts from his lectures and publications will be a nostalgic delight for those who encountered it first time round and will no doubt help to reinforce some enduring principles of good management for those to whom it is all new.

Institute of Leisure and Amenity Management

 BLAKE